# Ambitious Women Rise

## The Amazing Stories of Women Overcoming Obstacles and Creating the Life of their Dreams

Brenna Stanford

## Publishing History

Edition 1 / July 2021
ISBN: 978-0-557-94595-5
Imprint: Lulu.com

All Rights Reserved.

## Copyright @ 2021 Jessica Fox Coaching LLC, USA

No part of this book may be reproduced or transmitted in any form or by any means, electronic or mechanical, including photocopying, recording or any information storage and retrieval system, without permission in writing from the author.

# *Ambitious Women Rise*

# Dedications

To the women who are feeling buried and lost.
~ **Brenna Stanford**

I need to take a quick moment and thank my incredible husband Tyler for being the man of strength and compassion that he is, and for always believing in me and my dreams. To my many coaches and mentors in my life that have been a support, a sounding board, accountability and holding unwavering faith – I am forever grateful! Thank you!
~ **Jessica Fox**

This chapter is for my children, I see how I wasn't always there emotionally, and that you had to sometimes fend for yourselves because I was busy trying to grow up and be a better person. I pray you can forgive and heal the pain that my actions might have caused. To Todd Hartson, the one person who saw the beauty in me way before anyone could, including myself. Thank you for always believing in me and loving me anyway. To Alex, thank you for all the lessons and the one most critical lesson – loving myself. You will forever be in my heart. To my mother, I love you. You taught me how to be a "good person, to work hard, and to love anyway." And to all the angels that helped me along my journey, Paula, Megan O, Megan M, Cas, my sisters, Heather, Melanie, Azur, and the countless strangers, thank you for teaching me the lessons that I needed to see, hear and feel, and... HOWLING!
~ **Amanda Faye Hartson**

For Sara & Joana, mama loves you deeply!
~ **Catarina Rebelo**

For my husband, Jeff. My love, my friend and my biggest supporter. I WON'T LET GO!
For my stepdaughter, Anika. You are the reason I can be brave!
For my loving family, crazy friends, and amazing coworkers who have allowed me to try, fail, and grow!
Your support, wisdom, love, and presence has challenged me to be the best I can be.
~ **Erika**

# **Dedications**

To my family, my newborn son. To the women who choose to say YES every day.
**~ Dr. Izdihar Jamil, Ph.D.**

This is for Tony, told you I could do it!

To Abby and Pierre, Look at Mommy! ☺

And for my readers and students, Be who God created you to be – that is Your Authentic Self.
**~ LaMeshia Conley**

I dedicate this chapter to my mother, Sharon Elizabeth Jurd, for her unwavering faithfulness, resilience, sacrifices for her family, ministry of giving to anyone who crosses her path, and raising her children with values to overcome life's obstacles. Also, to every woman who is created in His image, I remind them, "You are enough."
**~ Megan Bruiners**

I dedicate my chapter to my father, Russell Thornton. Without his influence, strength, determination, and unfaltering support, I wouldn't be the woman I am today. Thanks to him for being a listening ear, a calm voice, a gentle heart, and most of all, a friend.

*Ambitious Women Rise*, but only due to those who lift them up.
**~ Mika Thornton**

Dear Josephine,
For the pain you've felt because of my unconscious patterns, I am sorry. I will spend the rest of my existence devoted to your healing. I love and adore you, unconditionally.
Love, Mama

A special thanks to Bekka Cardio and Ashley Newberg – the ones who've coached me through the toughest moments.

I am forever grateful to Sam, my amazing husband, for loving me for better or worse.
**~ Natalie Tellish**

To John, for authenticating our life's journey with love, integrity, humility, perseverance and to my children, Lauren, Carolina, Maria and Giaci, for guiding the way.
**~ Rita Miceli**

# Dedications

I would like to dedicate my chapter to my family and friends who have inspired and guided me to become the person I am today. I am blessed and forever grateful.
**~ Sara Ruda**

*Ambitious Women Rise*

# Book Reviews

"I saw myself in **Natalie**'s story. The pain of disconnection that I know all too well, the realization that the true disconnect is within myself, and the rise to a more conscious inner peace… Her experience is one of hope, and deep longings fulfilled in some of the most unexpected ways. I am inspired to get to know myself a little better today and reawaken 'the power within'."

~ **Ashley Newberg, Peaceful Parenting Coach at Like to Love Parenting**

WOW!!!! So very powerful!! I don't like reading, but I could have kept reading what **Natalie** wrote for hours. That sounds exactly like my life only I have yet to stop yelling or really start to work on healing as a mom. I really connected and felt drawn in and wanted to know more. Well done!!

~ **Heather Salivaras**

While reading this, I felt like I was reading a story of my life. It's so great to read something and realize that I'm not alone. This chapter gives me guidance on learning to consciously choose what I want to do to become better. Thank you for this, **Natalie**!

~ **Bonnie Yang**

**Rita Miceli** does a masterful job in describing the overwhelming stress she experienced, imposed from both without and within. Through her writing, the reader is able to understand, at a visceral level, how challenging raising a child with autism can be (particularly in the context of raising three other children at the same time). Such understanding is crucial for both extended families and educators at all levels connected to a family living with autism. Rita's eventual reconciliation with herself, and her acceptance of autism, can serve as a guide and a balm for other mothers (in particular), currently struggling with a child's recent autism diagnosis. With the benefit of hindsight Miceli is able to provide both perspective and guidance for families, not in "overcoming" autism, but in being able to live "with" autism and find joy.

~ **Elizabeth M. Starr, Ph.D., Professor Emerita, Faculty of Education, University of Windsor, Ontario, Canada.**

# Book Reviews

**Rita Miceli** has moved me beyond words. This introductory chapter is gripping, heartfelt, emotional, and real. Grappling with the challenges of a mother alone is relatable to so many of us, yet she shares her personal turmoil with the added pressures that come with one of her children having autism. Rita takes us through overwhelming feelings of despair in such a powerful way that I felt as though I was right there beside her. How many of us want to be invisible, put our own needs aside, and strive every day to do it all to our own detriment? Rita finds a way out of her own darkness after a terrifying experience, making conscious, intentional choices to leave her need for perfection behind.

Readers will be captivated by this journey of a family that finds a way to rise above each and every challenge through their unwavering love for each other.

~ **Lynn McLaughlin, Author**

**Rita Miceli**'s chapter will speak to so many mothers experiencing the challenges of parenthood, and especially to those experiencing the challenges that come with raising a child with autism. They will find hope in knowing they are not alone, and that their lives can still have purpose, and that they don't have to just identify as being a mother of a child with autism.

It will bring them hope that they can find their own identity again.

~ **Sarah Aldridge, Life Coach, Embrace the Shift, Leicester, UK**

**Rita Miceli**'s chapter, "My Perfect, Imperfect Life," is a powerful account of a woman's struggle to care for all of her children while desperately trying to unlock and enter the world of one. It is raw and authentic and is sure to tug at the heart strings of every mother.

~ **Dion Pandolfi, Nation Specialized Education Consultant, Michigan, USA**

Reading **Rita Miceli**'s chapter, "My Perfect, Imperfect Life," shares a rare glimpse into a mother's struggle to attain society's version of a perfect life after her son is diagnosed with autism. Walk alongside Rita as she discovers the imperfections of what perfect is, and how letting go allowed her to embrace all the joy and success she had been missing.

~ **Amy Seibel, Author of** *You're All Mine*, **Mother of one invigorating son, Occupational Therapist, and Educator, Ontario, Canada**

## *Ambitious Women Rise*

**Rita Miceli**'s beautifully written piece is a poignant portrayal of a mother's love for her children, and what every mother of an autistic child needs to read and read again. Rita provides her audience with a reflection of self- awakening, coming to terms with life being imperfect while cherishing those imperfections, and a realization that the love from a child is all that a mother needs and wants.

**~ Janet Bosnjak, OCT, Educator, Ontario, Canada**

This piece has brought a voice to the reality that so many mothers and their families have been silently facing for far too long. **Rita Miceli**'s vulnerability exemplifies a bold step in not just bringing awareness to the challenges faced by families raising individuals with ASD, but how to convert those challenges into gifts and opportunities to enrich society as a whole.

There is a lot we can learn from special populations and it is time we listened for that wisdom.

**~ Alex Waugh, Associate Pro Trainer, Chief Catalyst for Harmonized Health & Wellness, Ontario, Canada**

**Rita Miceli** did a great job highlighting how when we are left with ourselves, we think about all the negative thoughts that go through our heads about our own situations. This chapter made me smile, it made me chuckle, it made me tear up and most importantly it made me feel. Rita shares her vulnerability and her story that I think will help a lot of other families who have a child with autism.

**~ Sherrill Mallott, Life Coach, Ontario, Canada**

**Dr. Jamil**'s book is an inspirational read for all ambitious women who are ready to thrive beyond miracles with intentional simplicity.

**~ Arooj Ashraf, Business Growth Strategist**

**Dr. Izdihar Jamil**'s chapter is intriguing, truthful, and real!
**~ Pratibha Dey, Entrepreneur**

Magnificent read! **Dr. Jamil**'s writing is always so relatable, raw and authentic with powerful action steps.
**Emmy Hernandez, CEO Duality of Athena**

This was one of the rawest write-ups I've ever seen, very emotional. **Izdihar** shared her experiences so well that I felt I was having the moment with her.
**~Holly Lynn, Entrepreneur**

# Book Reviews

**Dr. Izdihar Jamil, Ph.D**, shared a story that many women can connect with. Balancing between motherhood and being a CEO can be a struggle, and finding the balance that works for you can be difficult. Dr. Jamil was able to share strategies that is can be easily implemented into your business model that allows you to step away without losing sales in your business.
~ **Sheng Herr, Business Strategist and Wealth Coach**

Real. Heartwarming. Encouraging. Challenging. And most of all, attainable!! **Brenna Standford**'s heart for the mothers led her to write this lovely book to let moms everywhere know we're not alone. And that with God's help, and a few of her tried and true "tricks of the trade", you can be (and already are) an empowered mom.
~ **Pastor Shinista Anderson, Pastor & Worship Leader at Life Church**

This is such an awesome book! I really love how **Brenna Standford** encouraged us to "create your circumstance!" Our lost, resilient, feelings oftentimes end up being the very purpose that keeps us going. When we aren't empowered or remember who we are in God, it affects so many other lives that we are joined to.
~ **Pastor Kym Tate, Pastor at Immanuel Fellowship Church**

**Catarina Rebelo**'s story relates to so many women around the globe who are waking up and discovering their inner power. Her five lessons are a powerful guide through awakening and discovering your purpose.
~ **Nevena Bazalac, High Performance Coach, Entrepreneur, and Author**

**Catarina Rebelo**'s story reveals an enormous personal growth, especially with regards to her awareness and commitment to what she really wants in her life.
The tips presented are the result of that, of her growth and evolution, and apply to anyone that just makes a commitment and really wants to evolve.
~ **Andreia Mendes**

## *Ambitious Women Rise*

Have you ever had your heart smile? I mean that feeling when your heart connects with something soul stirring, something sweet as honey, something so powerful and directive, that it ignites your heart to widen and disperse oxygen through every valve and chamber? That's what my heart did as I read **Megan Bruiners**' chapter, "There is purpose attached to your pain."

In this chapter, Megan captures the struggle of every woman that has dealt with self-doubt, diminished confidence, or battled rejection. She captures that woman with her own personal story of pain but then gives her the great plot twist! Woman of God, you weren't really captured, you've been free all along!

Megan reminds us that not only are we free, but we are also our greatest asset towards creating abundance. She paints a vivid picture of how pain can lead us to destiny, legacy, and being wealth creators.

Megan is a gifted writer and story teller. As you read this chapter, you will not only be motivated, but you'll gain the practical steps needed to move from past or present pain to purpose. And as you take those steps to move forward, I believe that your heart will smile. Mine sure did!

~ **Business Mindset Coach, Stephanie Nchege**

**Sara Ruda**'s story is a voice of inspiration to those who are in a dark place and don't see a way out. She is stronger than ever and as a co-worker I have seen how far she has come.

~ **Kaylie Kraft**

# *Ambitious Women*

## Table of Contents

Preface .................................................................................. xv

Arise in Empowered Purpose.......................................................1
   Brenna Stanford

Make the Choice and Chase Your Dreams..................................9
   Jessica Fox

Speak What You Want to See ....................................................17
   Alison Liddic

Forged in Fire............................................................................27
   Amanda Faye Hartson

How I Took Control of My Life Back From My Children .............37
   Amber Stephenson

From Feeling Helpless to Owning My Life .................................43
   Catarina Rebelo

A Journey to Me ........................................................................53
   Erika Olson

The New You..............................................................................59
   Dr. Izdihar Jamil, Ph.D.

Dare Not to Neglect Thyself.......................................................69
   LaMeshia Conley

Disruption to Destiny ................................................................79
   Megan Bruiners

Decision-Making to Decision-Acting..........................................89
   Mika Thornton

Consciously Rising ....................................................................97
   Natalie Tellish

My Perfect, Imperfect Life .......................................................105
   By Rita Miceli

It's Time to Take that Chance! .................................................115
   Sara Ruda

# *Ambitious Women Rise*

# Preface

## Ambition…

For many of us, the word "ambition" has become dirty word, evoking images of the demanding and impossible Miranda Priestly (*The Devil Wears Prada*), the successful editor-in-chief of a high-fashion magazine, who, while creating a culture of fear and striving among her staff, is watching her personal life fall apart as she is so driven to succeed, she has little time or presence for her family.

"Impossible" seems to be the correct word when we correlate try to the word "ambition" with women, not to mention "distasteful" for many.

But what if?

What if we reclaimed ambition? What if we allowed ambition to be a healthy drive and emotion? What if ambition could become a catalyst to rise above our circumstance and become the creators of our dreams and destinies?

Healthy ambition allows women to rise, and that is what this book is all about. Contained within these pages are the stories of women who have embraced their ambition and changed their life. Each one of these amazing women from all over the world has overcome obstacles in their lives and is now creating the life they have dreamed of. By embracing their ambition, they have truly risen to new heights and continue to rise, not only for themselves but for the sake of changing the lives of others.

Ambition need not be a dirty word. So, embrace your healthy ambition and let these women inspire you to truly live a life filled with freedom, purpose, and joy.

To your best life!

Jessica

## Ambitious Women Rise

## Brenna Stanford

*"Our deepest fear is not that we are inadequate. Our deepest fear is that we are powerful beyond measure. It is our light, not our darkness, that most frightens us. We ask ourselves, 'Who am I to be brilliant, gorgeous, talented, fabulous?' Actually, who are you not to be? You are a child of God. Your playing small does not serve the world. There is nothing enlightened about shrinking so that other people won't feel insecure around you. We are all meant to shine, as children do. We were born to make manifest the glory of God that is within us. It's not just in some of us; it's in everyone. And as we let our own light shine, we unconsciously give other people permission to do the same. As we are liberated from our own fear, our presence automatically liberates others."*
~ Marianne Williamson

# Arise in Empowered Purpose

## Brenna Stanford
## Empowered Moms Coach, USA

*"Our deepest fear is not that we are inadequate. Our deepest fear is that we are powerful beyond measure. It is our light, not our darkness, that most frightens us. We ask ourselves, 'Who am I to be brilliant, gorgeous, talented, fabulous?' Actually, who are you not to be? You are a child of God. Your playing small does not serve the world. There is nothing enlightened about shrinking so that other people won't feel insecure around you. We are all meant to shine, as children do. We were born to make manifest the glory of God that is within us. It's not just in some of us; it's in everyone. And as we let our own light shine, we unconsciously give other people permission to do the same. As we are liberated from our own fear, our presence automatically liberates others."*
~ Marianne Williamson

## Having More Happiness. Not Hating Life. Feeling Joy. Enjoying The Life That You Live.

These are the goals. Right?

These are things that we want. We want to speak and have conversations that are enjoyable and full of humor and love. We want to believe, really believe in the goodness that we've been told is out there for us. We know that God has goodness for us, but we aren't sure that we can actually live in it. We want to feel peace in our mind and not feel like we're drowning in thoughts that are yucky and constantly complaining. We want to know how to use the tools God has given us to live the abundantly free life He has given us. We know that it's not all rainbows and butterflies, but when the uncomfortable things come, doesn't that prove that we don't really have this goodness?

I get it – this internal struggle of trusting God and wondering how to live

## Brenna Stanford

this life in the flesh. How do I actually live these things out on a day-to-day basis? I hope that He really does have goodness for me, but I'm so unsure if I'll ever see it this side of heaven. There are so many circumstances to take into account, so many people, jobs, bills, variables all over the place. It all feels so unsettled, unsure. Well, if you have had those same questions, then I'm here to tell you that there is an answer. There is hope. There is an opportunity for you to arise and live in the more happiness, the real joy, the loving your life, and all the goodness that God has for you. And guess what? You can live in it this side of heaven too!

God led me on this journey long before I knew what we were doing. I felt hopeless in my life circumstances. I felt trapped and at the mercy of another. I knew that I needed a way out of the circumstance. However, being trapped brought out the survivor mode in me, and my mind raced with all the ways I could create a new circumstance. I would figure one out just to realize that the one needed was out of reach and impossible to achieve. Just on the other side of that very breath, that thought that I needed to make a way out of this circumstance, I knew that my existence was beyond the circumstances I felt trapped by. My conviction was to show the Love of Christ in that circumstance, show resilience and faithfulness. I knew I was to demonstrate belief, faith, and trust beyond measure – beyond what made sense. I knew that my purpose in those moments was to change the way I thought about those circumstances. I needed to stop seeing the bars that trapped me and begin praising God and declaring the freedom on the other side of the bars. That freedom felt like a wind that existed outside of those circumstances and within them all at once.

While the freedom wind comforted, I was still learning to see through my spirit. There were SO MANY DAYS that I spent crying, heaving under the weight of my tears and hopelessness. My eyes still saw so much of the reality that surrounded me. There were frustrations that had no answer. There were moments of circumstance that threatened my very life. There was only one way I could possibly relinquish the circumstance and make it through to the other side, to the freedom that blew in and through the bars of my circumstance.

Arise!


### Arise and Keep Going

Keep moving forward in faith. I knew that God would lead me. No matter what else was in play within the circumstance, I knew that I loved God and that He had my back, my front, my side, my above, my below – my everything. I knew that my children would be taken care of. His Word promised me that my children were sanctified by my faith. His Word promised me that He would never leave me. His Word promised me that He had a plan and a purpose for my life. His Word promised me that He has given me His authority to live and move and exist in. His Word promised me that He has given me His Holy Spirit to live with me in every moment.

So, I kept on, moving forward the only way that I knew how – one belief

## Arise in Empowered Purpose

at a time. In that moment, there was only one path I saw to journey on. So of course, I believed that the final deliverance into the freedom would be the success of that path. I became frustrated when the promise, the purpose, the freedom, didn't come when and how I thought it would. The circumstances that I felt trapped by, at times, were the things that gave me the resilience to keep going. I would look at them with the thought, *You won't get to hold me back much longer.* Then longer came. It seemed like everything was against me. I'd move forward, and the circumstance would get charged and flash like lightning, sometimes causing fires, sometimes knocking the power out, and at other times just showing me that it was there.

Every time I would stumble or fall, I would also arise. The power and Spirit of God inside of me would not let me stay down. To stay down was to forfeit life. Not just my life, but my husband's life, my children's life, and every person who knew me and knew the story of God that He had written with my life. I couldn't forfeit all of that. I continued to arise, trusting, knowing in my bones that at the exact right time, things would begin to shift. When God would be glorified the most in victory, that's when I would see it.

I didn't know that God was developing a warrior inside of me, that those flashes of lightning would seem like flickers of a candle. I didn't know that there was a woman inside of me who had been lost to that circumstance – a woman who was tired, a woman who was ready to finally say, "I'm done!" I didn't know that God was orchestrating the rhythm of His great plan to reveal itself in a thunderous boom, and that flashing light wouldn't flash to scare or torch or knock out the power, but that light would flash and reveal the truth that this plan and purpose was far greater than I could ever imagine.

**Sweet Woman, Whoever You Are, There Is a Warrior Inside of You.**

Under the tired, under the done, under the circumstances surrounding you, there is a warrior. God is orchestrating a rhythm in your life. At just the right moment, you will find that warrior woman arising into her true self. Do not give up.

Arise! Stand! Move forward!

Let go of the preconceived ideas about what it looks like. You may have imagined the promise and the purpose to look a specific way but remember that God is the God who is able to do all things exceedingly, abundantly, more than you can ask, think, or imagine. Keep your mind and heart open. Trust God that He will lead you, one step at a time, experiencing His grace and love through each step along your path. Let the flashes of lightning illuminate and shine so that you can see more clearly.

What the devil meant for evil; God meant for good. What was meant to knock out the power leaving you in darkness can now shine even more light in a single moment and show you things you didn't even know were there. What was meant to spark a fire and destroy can be the very fire that burns inside of you to give you warmth and light and energy. The warrior inside of you knows how to work with God in all things for your good and His glory.

That tension of trusting God and wondering how to live this flesh life out doesn't have to be exhausting and overwhelming. You don't have to struggle with every step you make. You don't have to worry about getting caught up in all the shoulds and should-nots. You get to live and move and breathe and exist in the presence of your Father Almighty and let His Holy Spirit lead you to make empowered choices in each moment. You won't get it all right, whatever "right" is. Not every little thing will be absolutely perfect and without fault. But I can promise you that this empowered life is perfect because even the <u>wrongs</u> become <u>right</u> with God when you allow Him to teach you lessons and make you better.

The uncomfortable things don't have to be a reminder that you don't actually have goodness. They can rather be the reminder that in ALL things, you have the Power and Spirit of God in you and with you to keep you moving forward, to keep you arising and standing as the empowered woman of God that you are! The choice is yours.

**Your Reading this Right Now Is Not a Coincidence**

This is a divine orchestration of the wonderful Father who loves you. This is the moment that His glorious thunder follows that flash of lightning and says, "Arise, daughter! I love you, and I have a great plan and purpose for you. Will you choose to journey with me?"

You may not know the destination, but you do know that there is a destination. You know that this arising empowers you. That your empowered life is about much more than you alone. You know that your empowered life is a vital part of the plan of eternity. Your empowered life is a light that flashes into the lives that you touch. Your empowered, arisen, flashing lightning allows the lightning that's flashing in their lives to be seen as giving of light and life, giving off warmth and energy instead of taking away power and light, causing a fire that scares and hurts.

You may never know all the lives that you touch and influence. You may never know the true impact of you arising into your empowered purpose has on the lives all around you. You see, God has this amazing way of catching attention. Just like us Okies (Oklahomans) are awe-inspired by a beautiful lightning show, the lightning show of your life will capture attention and inspire awe and wonder at the astounding power that charges your life and allows you to shine in such glory and magnificence. The moment that you choose to arise and step into your empowered purpose is the moment that heads turn, spirits take notice, the universe and all creation take notice and say, " There she is! There is the daughter of The King. There is the empowered woman warrior His Spirit has been calling out."

**You Get to Arise!**

Will you choose to arise and join me on this empowered journey? Will you

## Arise in Empowered Purpose

choose to answer the call of the Holy Spirit and walk with me and all of your sisters on this amazing journey? Your arising not only catches the attention of the world around you, but this moment of decision is the moment that captures the warrior inside you. Choosing this simple yet critical act is what is setting you on the path of empowered purpose.

Take a moment and ask yourself a few questions...
- If nothing changes, where will I be in five years? Where will my family be in five years if nothing changes?
- If I choose to arise and step into this empowered purpose, no matter how unknown it may feel right now, where will I be in five years? Where will my family be in five years?

Answer those questions and find the truth in your heart – then choose.

Stand and arise with me. Step into your empowered purpose and cause all creation around you to erupt in praise and cheer as they stand and watch awe-inspired by the warrior woman inside of you.

Keep moving forward, wonderful, empowered, arisen woman!

*Brenna Stanford*

Brenna Stanford

# Brenna Stanford

## About the Author

My name is **Brenna Stanford** and I love helping overwhelmed moms create their Empowered Motherhood! No matter how your days are filled, finding the best balance and learning how to take care of yourself is vital!

I am a daughter of The King, wife to Zack, and mother of Keegan, Zachery, Lucille, and Jedidiah. I am the founder of Empowered Motherhood: Happy Mom Hacks & Mindset Tools and the signature PAM system, author of *Just Two Minutes: A Devotion for Busy Moms*, and a Moms Empowerment Coach. I had been in a ministry inside a church for ten years when I came home to be a stay-at-home mom. I have helped moms from all around the world to create their Empowered Motherhood!

I absolutely love to have coffee dates and oily gatherings! I proclaim that I am fueled by Jesus, oils, and coffee. Worship music is my favorite, but I've been known to embarrass my kids by bustin' out and rapping along with whatever is playing on the house FM – but don't ask me to dance! No one wants to see that!

My heart lights up when I get to chat with you wonderful ladies about your life, current circumstances, and your deepest desires! I believe in every fiber of my being that there is an empowered warrior inside of you waiting to arise and make a difference in your world.

# Arise in Empowered Purpose

## Find Me!

**Brenna Stanford**
EMPOWERING MOMS

**Grab your Free Happy Mom Hacks:**
https://www.brennastanford.us/3-happy-mom-hacks

**Get More Great Gifts and Free Resources at:**
https://www.facebook.com/groups/empoweredmotherhood1

**Connect with me on *Facebook*, *Instagram*, and *Clubhouse* –** @BrennaStanford

**Email:** brennastanfordpro@gmail.com

**Website:** www.brennastanford.us

# Make the Choice and Chase Your Dreams

## Jessica Fox
## Master Transformation Coach, USA

*"The future belongs to those who believe in
the beauty of their dreams."*
~ Eleanor Roosevelt

### Hitting Rock Bottom

"You have two choices: filing for bankruptcy or insolvency."

I sat across a large, beautiful desk as she explained my options. I glanced out the windows of the downtown high-rise, and I was overwhelmed by the gloom of the day and the hopeless situation I was in. The guilt, the shame, the embarrassment, and the sense of failure were overwhelming. I could hardly concentrate on the information being shared. After losing my health, career, and income, I didn't believe I could sink any lower.

I was wrong.

I was thirty-four years old with two children and one on the way. My husband was struggling to keep a roof over our heads. I hadn't worked in over a year due to illness. Now we were facing the reality that we may lose our home and vehicles on top of everything we had lost the previous year. I thought I had already hit rock bottom when I burned out of my career, and here I was, even lower, facing even more devastating consequences. The weight of my reality was so heavy that I just sat in that office and cried. Clearly, the agent was used to this response and had tissues ready. She graciously waited in reassuring silence while I worked through my emotions.

I left the office in defeat, having signed the papers that would get the creditors off our backs while allowing us to keep our home. I sat down in my car and began to sob, and that grief quickly turned to anger. My anger at the situation, anger at myself, anger at God. The anger exploded out of me in a fury of yelling at my steering wheel:

# Jessica Fox

"Why is this happening to us?"
"Life is supposed to be better than this!"
"What did we do wrong?"
"Why can't anything go right?"
"I can't do this anymore!"
"What's the point of any of this?"

My anger exhausted and feeling hopeless and dejected, I made my way home from my appointment, embarrassed and alone.

## I Had Become a Victim

A week or so after the shock of signing insolvency papers had worn off, my husband and I sat down to figure out how we would manage our monthly payments and have the hard conversation about how we had gotten into the situation and circumstances we were facing. Through our discussion, we noted that some of our circumstances were out of our control, some came because we followed misguided advice, and some were the result of poor decision-making on our part. But rather than taking responsibility and looking for solutions, I developed a "Why me?" attitude. I became a victim of my circumstances, blaming everyone and everything for the situation we were facing. I was angry, and at the same time, I felt defeated and wondered if our life would ever change. The truth here is that I had taken on this victim role more than once in my life. While it felt completely disempowering to be a victim, I didn't actually realize that is what I was doing – until now!

## Enough was Enough

The weeks following filing insolvency awakened me to the fact that I had been playing the victim to the circumstances of my life. It was like a thick fog suddenly lifted from my heart and brain, and I could see the consequences that playing the victim had not only in my external world but on my internal one.

With the fog of "Why me?" lifted, I could see how I had surrendered my personal power and my responsibility to be the creator of my own life. I could see how far I had strayed from my sense of purpose and how I had lost belief in the beauty of my dreams. I knew at that moment that I had a choice: to continue playing the victim or take back my dreams, my power, and control as the creator of my life.

Enough was enough, and I chose to take my power back!

## The Revelations

I would love to tell you that leaving victimhood, reclaiming my dreams, and stepping into my power was as easy as flipping a light switch, but it wasn't. I had developed habits of thought, belief, and behavior that served my victim mindset. It took time, effort, determination, and the intentional re-programming

## Make the Choice and Chase Your Dreams

of my mind with the help of both a coach and counselor to me get back to the woman I knew I was and desired to be again. There were several revelations of truth that I learned as I healed and recommitted to my true self that I want to share with you right now.

### Revelation 1: Self-Forgiveness is Necessary

I cannot stress how important forgiving yourself is when you realize that you have allowed yourself to slip into victimhood. Self-forgiveness is the first step that creates internal space for you to take back your personal power. Even more so, if you are reading this and realize that, maybe, you have been playing a victim of your life and circumstances longer than you would like to admit. Getting caught up in the circumstance of life is something we have all experienced to one extent or another, but we have a choice. We can choose to experience more out of life. We can choose to learn from our circumstances and create new opportunities rather than succumb to them. We can choose to forgive ourselves for the ways we have fallen short, letting go of the past, and we can choose to embrace a better future.

### Revelation 2:    Everything is "    Figureoutable"

Marie Forleo says:

> "No matter what you're facing, you have what it takes to figure _anything_ out and become the person you're meant to be. You wouldn't have the dream if you didn't already have what it takes to make it happen."

You need to read that again! You wouldn't have the dream if you didn't already have what it takes to make it happen. Even though you may feel like you've lost your sense of self or lost the belief that your dreams could come true, you need to know that because you have the dreams you have, they are yours to realize in this life. When you step into your power and go from "I can't!" to "How can I?" the way to realize the dream and vision you have for your life will open to you. Your dreams are not lost, they are absolutely figureoutable!

### Revelation 3: What You Think, You Create

Whatever you choose to believe about yourself and your circumstance is true. If you believe it is a learning opportunity that can change your life for the better, it is. If you believe it is just evidence that nothing ever goes right and nothing will change, it is. For good or bad, what you think and what you put your mental energy towards will come to pass in your life. We always have a choice: Will I be a victim of my circumstance and perpetuate a victimized existence, or will I put the power of my thoughts to work and create a better future for me to experience? When we understand the reality of this statement,

# Jessica Fox

"What I think, I create," it puts into motion the desire for constructive, life-giving thinking that transforms our lives in remarkable ways.

## Revelation 4: Anchors Are a Must

One of the strategies I teach all my clients is to anchor their commitment to their vision, dreams, and goals with something in the physical environment that is triggered by the five senses. It could be a song, a smell, a picture, or a phrase. The anchor should be meaningful, powerful, and somewhere accessible. The purpose of this anchor is to help keep you focused and to help you when you slip back into those old habits of thought and belief. By using anchors throughout the process of reclaiming your dreams and your personal power, you are setting yourself up for success by reminding yourself of who you truly are and the life you desire to have.

## Revelation 5: Recommit to Your Dream and Vision

The choice to no longer be a victim to your circumstances and step back into your personal power needs to be followed by a recommitment to a dream and vision you have for your life. For some, it's about creating a dream and vision that you've never allowed yourself to have before. For others, it's reconnecting and fanning into flame the embers of a dream that was almost extinguished. What is amazing in this process is that the spark of dreams and visions quickly transforms into a burning desire, and with a burning desire comes energy, intention, direction, and focus.

As I began to implement the lessons I learned from those five revelations and really allowed my sense of purpose, passions, and dreams to begin directing my choices, my life very quickly turned around. And here I am today, writing this chapter as proof that when you let go of being a victim and step into your power, dreams really do come true.

## Dreams Do Come True

In a way, it is almost surreal how different my life is now from the day I cried and screamed in defeat at my steering wheel. I reconnected with my heart and purpose to empower women, and now I get the privilege of serving hundreds of entrepreneurial moms as a Master Transformational Coach and by launching the Thriving Business Mamas Movement. I have recently moved into the house of my dreams, and in less than a year, I had the honor of fulfilling a lifelong dream of not only becoming a published author but becoming an international bestselling author with two more titles being released on the heels of the first. I also had the privilege of being a featured on a *TED-Ed* stage, and all of this during a pandemic.

I look at how quickly my life changed with a sense of awe and profound gratitude, and I know it is because I made a choice – a choice to embrace my power and purpose, follow my dream and vision, and go for it! The result, you, dear reader, are experiencing with me, in this moment, today.

# Make the Choice and Chase Your Dreams

## Inspired Actions

If you are ready to make the choice and make your dreams a reality, I have a few simple, implementable action steps for you to consider.

1. **Create a Plan.** Once you choose to let go of the victim mentality, it is so important to know where you desire to go. Know the big picture. Know what you desire to experience in this life and align yourself, your belief, and your actions with the outcome you desire to experience in this life. Even if you don't know how you will get from where you are to where you want to be, creating the plan and trusting the process will produce fruit in your life that is better than you could have ever imagined.

2. **Surround Yourself with the Right People.** For better and for worse, the people in our life influence our mindset, our decisions, our confidence, and direction. Make sure to surround yourself with those that believe in the dream that you are holding for your future and ones that will call you out of playing a victim when less than ideal circumstances come your way. Your community, friends, and mentors need to hold you to the dreams and potential you have been created to experience. So, don't settle for less when it comes to the people you surround yourself with.

3. **Own your Personal Power.** We only have one life, and we might as well make it our best. Recognize that when you live in a mindset or heart-set that is less than the fullness of your purpose, power, and potential, you won't experience all that this life has to offer. So, don't settle for anything less and walk as who you have been created to be – the only you that will ever walk on and change this amazing world.

## Jessica Fox

You can do this! This is your life! These are your dreams! It is your future!

Make your choice today and live this life to the fullest.

> *No matter what you're facing, you have what it takes to figure anything out and become the person you're meant to be. You wouldn't have the dream if you didn't already have what it takes to make it happen.*
> *~ Marie Forleo*

# Make the Choice and Chase Your Dreams

## About the Author

**Jessica Fox** is blazing a trail for ambitious women.

You may have caught her on *NBC*, *CBS*, *FOX*, and the *CW*. She is a master coach, a three-time bestselling author, and has been interviewed on *TED-Ed*.

Jessica has worked with organizations such as the Flames NHL Hockey team, the Stampeders Canadian football team, Subway, and Starbucks.

Jessica has thousands of hours teaching and training from the stage and in intimate settings.

She has helped ambitious moms hit consistent $10,000 sales months, go from laid off to signing a six-figure contract within three months, and produced $53,000 in team sales in the first month working together.

Most days, you will find her in her comfiest jeans or yoga pants, enjoying good coffee and lost in her never-satisfied book addiction.

Originally from Canada, Jessica makes her home in northwest Arkansas, just a few miles from Walmart's headquarters, with her husband Tyler and their three amazing children.

# Jessica Fox

# Find Me!

If having a breakthrough in your business and motherhood is something that interests you, please check out my links below.

**Grab your copy of *Yes I Can!* here:** https://bit.ly/36c44W5

**Check out my *TED-Ed* feature here:** https://bit.ly/3lb2FFr

**Book your Free Pathway to Thrive Breakthrough Session:**
https://jessicafox.ca/timewithjess

**Receive your Free Gift, The Ambitious Woman's Guide to Thrive:**
https://bit.ly/3aysfQB

**Join my *Facebook* Group:** https://bit.ly/thrivingWAHMs

*LinkedIn*: www.linkedin.com/in/jessicafoxcoaching

*Instagram*: https://www.instagram.com/thethrivingbusinessmama/

*Email*: jessicafoxcoaching@gmail.com

# Speak What You Want to See

## Alison Liddic
### Business Focus Coach, USA

*I didn't want to claim it because I was
doubting His power and His will for me,
but I heard the Holy Spirit say,
"If you want to see it, you need to speak it
and you need to speak it now."*
~Alison Liddic

**There I was, 38 years old, ...**

...standing at the bottom of the stairs, wondering how I would make it to the top. Every step up the steps filled my body with severe pain that started from inside my bones and worked its way out. I had over 30 different health symptoms and no answers from anyone. Nothing helped. My bones ached; I had the feeling of a fever every day but never had a temperature. Each day came with different levels of headaches, but there was rarely a day without one.

But I did as any woman would do, and I pushed through; I did what I needed to do. I'd cake on the makeup to try to cover up my gray complexion

## Alison Liddic

and my dark circles. I'd tease my hair to try to cover up where my hair was falling out. I put on my fake happy face and went on with my day. I was at the point where I thought this was how I was going to have to live. This was just my new normal.

Each night when I was trying to fall asleep, I wasn't sure if I would wake up the next day. I got to the point where I was okay with that.

I went to doctor after doctor and had test after test in every lab you can think of! Yet every outcome was "Everything is great!" – but I wasn't great.

Why was every test normal, yet I felt like I was dying? For real, dying! At 38 years old, I felt more like 95!

I threw up my hands and cried out to the Lord. This became my focus in my prayer time. I was asking for answers about my health and was praying for healing. And boy did he answer!

While scrolling through *Instagram* one day, the Lord led me to a hashtag I had never seen before. It was for something called "Breast Implant Illness." What in the actual world is "Breast Implant Illness"?

Wait, I have breast implants... And, I have an "illness" that couldn't be identified. Could this be my answer?

It was like a giant lightbulb moment for me. Of course, I began digging. I checked the common symptom list, and I had ALL but three of them!

For 12 years, my health had been declining, and I was never, ever told that it could be linked to my breast implants. Never! After reading a TON and praying even more, I moved forward with getting my implants removed. It was quite a process to find a surgeon that does the en bloc total capsulectomy that is needed. I spent an entire day calling every doctor on this entire list to find a surgeon that could get me in the fastest. Time was truly not on my side.

In the meantime, my life was crazy being a top sales rep in the medical device industry. I would travel almost weekly and was responsible for at least ten states in the US and for hitting big quotas. It was a lot of stress but was always something I was able to handle.

This was something I had done for over ten years, so it should be okay, right? I could handle it, right? Maybe if I just kept pushing through – put on my fake face to hide the severe pain that I was feeling every single day.

My fatigue got to the point where I couldn't get through a day without a nap, and I never felt rested. Every trip I went on for work left me so swollen!

# Speak What You Want to See

Inflammation was at a new level for me, and since I had to travel every week, I didn't have enough time to recover before the next flight. It was an endless cycle that was spiraling my health way down. Not only could I not be there physically and emotionally for myself, but I couldn't be there for my kids or my husband. I was missing out on life, watching it happen around me as I laid in my bed trying to recover. It was like I was trapped! Prisoner in my own body, and I couldn't get out.

I had another decision to make. Even though I was the main provider for our family, I decided to quit my job and focus on getting well.

This was such a hard decision for me! I've never just quit a job without having another one to step directly into. I quit my job and now somehow have to come up with $6K+ to pay to have my breast implants removed. What was I thinking?

A host of thoughts were coming at me. I was sick because I decided to modify my body by getting breast implants, so it was my fault. I was letting my employer down by turning in my notice. I was letting my family down, taking away my income and our health insurance. I felt like a complete failure.

And at this point, I wasn't even sure if it was the breast implants making me sick. What if it wasn't? Then what? What if I spend all this money, and it doesn't even work?

**That Was the Moment when Everything Changed**

God used this time to speak into me and build my faith. He asked me, "Alison, are you waiting to claim your healing until after your surgery? Because if so, that tells me that you don't believe in who I am and what I can do for you."

Wow! Well, God sure called it like it was. I was just waiting to see if He could..., if He would heal my body. I didn't want to claim it because I was doubting His power and His will for me. I heard the Holy Spirit say, "If you want to see it, you need to speak it and you need to speak it now."

That moment, I got out my computer, prayed, and started a *Facebook Live* session. Most people I know had no clue I even had implants. I was dealing with a TON of shame and condemnation about putting that out into *Facebook* space. What would people think of me? But I did it anyway.

I started by sharing how I've been feeling. I showed the file folder of all my medical tests over the last 12 years. Then, I spoke about breast implant illness and how I believe that is what is making me sick. I also SPOKE about

## Alison Liddic

how God was already healing mem and that I believed I would be completely healed.

The *Live* session ended.

What happened after that was truly heartwarming. Not only did I get tons of love, but I got TONS of messages from women dealing with the same health issues. And guess what? They had implants too! They had no idea it could be connected. I also had people reach out to see if they could contribute financially to my surgery! Really? Someone would want to do that?

I was truly mind blown by the love and support!

Very long story short... I flew from Ohio to West Palm Beach, FL, to have my surgery just a few months later. My amazing husband was by my side the entire time, taking care of my every need.

After a few months of taking it easy, I was able to start crossing symptoms off my list. I was getting better!! I went from over 30 symptoms down to just two!

**Our Reality**

As women, as mothers, we can push through pretty much anything life throws at us. Depending on the circumstance, this can be good, or this can be bad. I lived my life for 12 years just pushing my health issues to the side – dealing with the headaches, dealing with the bloating, dealing with chronic inflammation. I could go on and on.

This was putting a huge strain on me. It was impacting my relationship with friends because I couldn't go out anymore. It was impacting my relationship with my kids because I couldn't take them anywhere. It was impacting my relationship with my husband on many levels, and it was putting a huge strain on my relationship with my heavenly Father.

I mean, when life throws us lemons, we women, we make some killer lemonade! Am I right?

We do what we can with the bad situation we are in.

But I heard something recently that changed my perspective of this. What if I don't want lemonade? What if I want orange juice?

I don't want to have to accept the lemons that are thrown at me! I want to throw them back and get some juicy oranges instead!

# Speak What You Want to See

## Determined Decisions Change Circumstances

I had to sit and reflect. What lemons have I just accepted that I never wanted?

- **Lemon** – Your body doesn't look right; change your body.
- **Lemon** – You don't feel good, but you look fine, so you must be alright.
- **Lemon** – You have to hustle and grind if you ever want to change your life financially.
- **Lemon** – True success is climbing the corporate ladder as fast as possible.

**Lies!!!**

I made the decision to toss those lemons right out of my life! I started by forgiving myself for getting implants in the first place. Then, I forgave myself for now having a scarred body. I then forgave myself for giving up almost 20 years of my life to hustle and grind to rise to the top to prove myself to everyone else.

I chucked those lies so far out of my life I probably hit the Atlantic!

I made the decision that even though I was better now, I was NOT going back to work. I was not going to leave my family every single week again now that I was finally able to live.

God started speaking into me and putting desires into my heart, new desires that I didn't know what to do with. He gave me a heart for women. He spoke to me about my true identity in Christ and asked me to teach others the same. He placed women in my life to coach in their business. He asked me to start not one but TWO podcasts.

Because I said NO to going back to work, I was able to start saying YES to the things he had for me. I was able to officially start my own coaching business, something I could have never done while I was sick. My life was completely transformed!

None of this would have happened if I hadn't been sick & if I didn't quit my job.

My question for you: What lemons have you just accepted? What areas in your life are you trying to make lemonade when all you want is fresh orange juice? And what could change in your life if you were willing to toss those lemons back?

## My Hard-Knock Lessons to Live By

### Lesson 1: Don't neglect to pray for yourself!

My prayer times were all about everyone else. When it came to the time to pray for me, I would just skip on over that. God has so much to worry about. He doesn't have time to listen to me complain about my aches and pains.

Not true!! He loves you and cares about you. He wants you to live life and live it more abundantly! So, talk to the Father about your needs. He cares for you.

### Lesson 2: Don't accept someone else's diagnosis and your final answer.

Listen, ladies! I'm pretty sure we have a superpower to know when something isn't right. You know your body, your kids, your spouse. If you don't feel right, don't accept it as normal. Start digging until you find the answer because trust me, you will find it!

Ask God to show you and put in the effort to get some answers. Just because it was a diagnosis doesn't mean it's your destiny. You have the power to change it.

### Lesson 3: If you want to see it, you must SPEAK it!

God really gave me a gut punch by showing me that I was full of doubt, not by what I was speaking but by what I wasn't speaking. I wasn't fully believing, so I wasn't speaking it. Our words have so much power!

Look around. What do you see? You are seeing what you have spoken at some point in your life. What we speak becomes reality, so shift your words and start speaking what you want to see.

I wanted healing, so I had to claim "HEALED!", not "*will be* or *could be* healed, but "HEALED!"

### Lesson 4: If you don't like lemonade, throw the lemons back!

Just to clarify, I'm not asking you to be negative about your situation. I'm asking you to realize the power that you have. You don't have to accept things as they come your way. You have the power to say "NO!", it isn't going to be this way and do the work to change it. Through prayer and action, you will start to see a shift.

# Speak What You Want to See

Ask God to show you where you've accepted lemons. Maybe he wanted you to have orange juice, and your friend or your mom tossed in a lemon, and you took your eye off the orange. Toss out the lemons and create the life you want.

Don't settle!

## My Breakthrough

The process I went through completely changed my life. I can't even say I was healed; I feel more like a completely new person. God filled me with creative energy and put me to work making a Kingdom impact.

I could have easily healed and went back into sales and never thought twice. But because I gave God room to speak into me, I was able to follow His direction.

Now I get to work with women every single day to help them in their businesses and realize how amazing they are. God gave us the example of the woman in Proverbs 31 how He does not do things shame us or intimidate us, but to inspire us. God is not a respecter of persons. If he did it for her, I knew He can do it for me. I just had to make myself available and make room for him to use me.

It is a next-level joy to see a woman step into her greatness – to be the woman she was created to be, to be living in pure joy and peace while running a successful business and raising kids! I am honored that God chose me to do this type of Kingdom work!

He did it for the Proverbs 31 woman. He's doing it for me. He's doing it for my clients.

He can do it for you!!

> *"Don't just make the best of your situation. Change it! Don't settle for lemons if you hate lemonade. Speak what you want to see and take the action to make it happen."*
> ~ Alison Liddic

Go make a Kingdom impact, sister!

**Let's do this!**

# Alison Liddic

Alison Liddic

# Speak What You Want to See

## About the Author

Hey, everyone! I'm **Alison Liddic**, owner of Alison Liddic Coaching. I get to work with Christian women running their businesses and trying to do it all in life! I am a wife of 19 years to my amazing husband, Tony, and mom of three beautiful teenage girls. I have an unhealthy love of coffee... Oh, and anything Rae Dunn... Seriously, all of it!

My PASSION and purpose are helping Christian Women FLOURISH in business and life, AND to learn how to have a supernatural focus on God's plan for their business giving them more time, joy, and confidence!

It's an honor to get to coach women from ALL OVER!

# Alison Liddic

# Find Me!

**If you are a Christian woman** who has a business or has always wanted to start a business, come join my free *Facebook* group:
Flourishing Business Without Overwhelm

**Follow me on** *Facebook* **at**: Alison Liddic VIP

**Connect with me on** *LinkedIn*: https://www.linkedin.com/in/alisonliddic/

I'd also like to offer a free deep dive into your business to talk strategy! Visit my website and click **Let's Talk!**
https://alisonliddic.com/

# Forged in Fire

## Amanda Faye Hartson
## Realtor, USA

*"Forged in fire, from the ashes, I will rise!."*
~ Unknown

Women wear many hats in life. We try to be all things to everyone: wife, mother, sister, daughter, friend, lover, professional…, the list goes on *ad infinitum*. We go through life trying to be better than what we were yesterday. In the process, sometimes, we end up losing who we truly are, trying to be something we are not, only to make others happy. Self-deprecating? NO! In fact, it's defiling ourselves – settling for less to be more. We are all walking contradictions, running through life, missing the mystery, the sweet kiss of truth and happiness. The enigma exists beneath the surface, buried deep down under all the rubble of daily duties of being who we think we should be, defiling ourselves every day.

The answer to the riddle remains unknown. We hear the mystery call out to us, yearning for us to listen to our bones, to be true to our souls, but, instead, we close our eyes to our truth, hoping for something better, waiting for something to change so we can be who we are without faking it, or feeling like we should be something we are not.

I write this chapter to be a beacon of hope for any woman who is struggling with becoming her authentic self. I believe that everyone's definition of success is different, and my story is not about money, what I drive, where I live, or who I know. Success, to me, is not tangible or external. It is about internal peace. It is about waking up, being present in my daily life, being connected to source, God, Mother Mystery, or whatever you feel comfortable calling your Higher Power. It is about being connected and being true to myself. If I am connected and staying true to myself and to God, well…, all the external, monetary things just happen for me and continue to happen for me.

My journey of becoming my authentic self-started over 28 years ago. Coming from generations of motherless children and being forced to grow up at an incredibly young age, I, too, became a mother at 18 and battled with the question, *Who am I?* Unfortunately, I was also battling addiction to anything and everything that allowed me to ignore the emptiness I felt inside my soul. Shopping, food, sex, drugs, 'n rock-n-roll! Nothing was excluded. I welcomed it wholeheartedly, as long as it numbed the ache of being alone in a room full of people, my feeling of being the outcast, or, better yet, the ugly duckling. Never belonging anywhere but being everywhere.

People would tell me how beautiful I was, and I would laugh to myself and think, *If they only knew what was inside, if they could see me, they wouldn't love me or think I was beautiful.* As a child, I remember when people would complement me and tell me that I was "pretty," my mother would say, "Pretty is what pretty does." Not until I was an adult did I understand why she would whisper that to me. I honestly thought she was cutting me down, but little did I know, she was trying to teach me a valuable lesson. Socrates said,

> "Give me beauty in the inward soul; may the outward and the inward man be at one."

I could not see the beauty outside because I felt ugly inside. However, I believe that God has always been with me, guiding me, watching and patiently waiting for me to see the truth – my truth.

**Synchronicities – The Beginning**

Twenty-eight years ago, I was running away again, needing to be anywhere but where I was at the time. Seven hundred miles from home, I went to the mall to grab some things that I needed, but instead of going where I wanted, I was guided into a bookstore by something larger than myself. Without thinking, I walked straight to a book as if I were being pulled there. The book was *Women Who Run with the Wolves* by Clarissa Pinkola Estes. As I took the book from the shelf, I turned around, and on a chair beside the shelf, I saw a blanket with the serenity prayer on it. I bought both!

In her book, Clarissa talks about "La Loba," the old one who waits for lost and wandering people to come to her place, especially those that are in danger of being lost in the world. It reads,

> "If you are lucky, La Loba may take a liking to you and

# Forged in Fire

*show you something of the soul."*

Her words touched me at my very core. Words cannot do justice to the feelings I had, and I will fail miserably. Now you may think I am crazy, but I know something MUCH BIGGER than myself brought me to that very mall, that very bookstore, and guided me to that very book. I could hear all the women before me who were once as lost as I was as if they were speaking to me from the grave,

> *WAKE UP, AMANDA FAYE, DON'T RUN, FACE YOURSELF. Be the wild woman you were created to become!*

The next day, I did not run away, and I drove back home. It was the beginning of my journey of finding real happiness. I decided to stay for the very first time in my life, to participate in the life that was being offered to me, and to start my journey of facing my truth and healing the emptiness inside.

## My Angel – Facing the Truth

Several years later, although I had made some decisions and started to create a life beyond party Amanda. I was still struggling with the emptiness inside, battling in my mind, right and wrong, which path to take, trying to be everything to everyone and failing miserably, but worst of all, failing myself. I do not know how to explain how I met this person, but I will say when I met her, I said, "I was supposed to meet you." Of course, she laughed at me, smirked, and said, "Yeah, right, you won't call me."

Now you do not know me, but there is one attribute that I have always had and has served me well – tenacity or some would argue, stubborn as hell! Naturally, I made it a point to call her the very next day. Megan showed me how to be honest with myself, even when it was extremely hard. Now, one might say and undoubtedly believe that they are being honest with themselves. I would still be asleep to the lies I told myself if it were not for her. I mean, how do you know until you know?

We are taught from the beginning of our birth, call it patriarchal ideology or domestication if you must, but women are taught that we are supposed to be a certain way, and if we are not, we are bad. You may not resonate with the story I am telling you. Still, the best way to know if you are not living authentically, is to ask yourself, *Am I genuinely happy or does my soul long for something different?*

Whether it be in a relationship or a career choice, it does not matter. If

## Amanda Faye Hartson

you feel like you are not whole, then something is not right inside.

While I was working with Megan, a book and writer was brought to my attention – *The Invitation* by Oriah Mountain Dreamer. In this book she wrote,

> *"If you can bear the accusation of betrayal and not betray your own soul. If you can be faithless and therefore trustworthy."*

This is the absolute truth. Sometimes we are pulled in a direction that requires us to break agreements with people, and it hurts! But what is worse, temporary pain or discomfort of not knowing what we are going to be or how we are going to provide for our family, or a lifetime of regret? I asked myself that very question many years ago, and I chose a life of the unknown. I jumped from the proverbial cliff and said, "Geronimo!" What I heard and understood with this prose in her poem was, if I am true to myself and make decisions based on my soul and my connection to God, I can be trustworthy. Of course, I must remember that this rule applies to me as well. If someone that I love needs to find something beyond me, if I do not fill their soul's needs, I too may get hurt. Now that was a tough pill to swallow.

I know, now, that it was not my choice. I had to let go and let him find his own path and, from a distance, love him anyway.

### Break Through a Break Down

Sometimes, however, it is hard to see the forest for the trees. And as soon as your ego is involved, unfortunately, you can slip back into disillusionment once again. This point brings me to my third spiritual experience, one that was incredibly difficult to see, and it took a bartender to help me uncover my truth.

During the last 28 years of finding who I am authentically by practicing forgiveness, love, and integrity, I also spent a lot of money on my education. I would boast about being a professional student, and I took a lot of pride in what I did for my career. I worked for a well-known financial firm and made excellent money. I thought I had made it! I had arrived! Little did I know, God had other plans for me.

I enjoyed a decent tenure as a financial advisor. However, due to some unfortunate circumstances, some made by my own choices and some outside of my control, I was forced to make a career change. This three-year battle with myself and my ego almost drove me to financial ruin. I was forced

## **Forged in Fire**

to move back into my mother's home. Can you imagine? The humility of it! Ha! Ha! Ha!

Once I moved in with my mother, I had to swallow my pride and look for a job that would help pay the bills until I could get the training I needed for my next endeavor. I had to become a waitress. As I was sitting at the bar, waiting for the manager, mortified that I was forced to lower my standards to get a job, blaming everyone and everything around me, praying to God that nobody walked in and saw me interviewing to be a waitress. As a distraction, I started talking to the bartender. Of course, I had to explain to her that I was a financial advisor, give her the details of my education, and the litany of excuses of why I had to leave the industry. She looked at me, shrugged her shoulders and smiled, "Well, my parents don't like what I do, but I make incredible money, and I am happy."

Let me add that she is the bar manager of a craft beer and food restaurant, in a popular, bourgeois area and probably makes six figures a year. I was like, "Wow! What do they care if you are happy?" When I heard those words come out of my mouth, it was an instant "Ah ha!" moment! Thunder and lightning crashed, and the Angels sang.

I had to laugh at how ridiculous I had been over the last few years, struggling with the idea of who I was going to be if I was not a financial advisor. All my identity had been wrapped up in such a tiny little package! Then, I remembered who I was, and remembered the lesson my mom instilled in me many years ago, "May the internal woman be at one."

I was happy, even living with my mom and interviewing for a job as a waitress. I also remembered Wayne Dyer and his book, *The Power of Intention*. He talks about the ego and not living in line with spiritual principles and the internal consequences of it. He wrote,

> *"The problem is when you misidentify who you truly are by identifying yourself as your body, your achievements, and your possessions..."*

That very instant, I let go and let God take control. Over the last two years, I had been figuring out who Amanda Faye truly is, searching for the very essence of my being. I had died a thousand deaths – professionally, spiritually, physically (heart), and mentally – and by the Grace of God and His Power, I still rise, like the Phoenix rising from the ashes, developing each new chapter of my life, closer and closer to living authentically and being whole. The universe or my higher power has always brought me little nuggets of truth, synchronicities, either through people (my Angels) or

## Amanda Faye Hartson

through literature. However, the "forged in fire" is a lesson that I have had to learn SOOO many times throughout the years – learning things the hard way, fighting battle after battle, sifting through the ashes, rising again and again, smarter, wiser from the pain I created, just to turn and do it all over again.

In this new chapter, I am making myself another promise, to stay awake, to shed the idea of the Phoenix rising, and to turn to the wild woman that was brought to me over 28 years ago, "La Loba." I also I know I need to be aware, to look before I leap, to step back and sit with the questions, to stay connected to source, and to keep shining even when things are "not going my way..."

### Who Is Amanda?

I am where I am supposed to be today, I do not think it is a coincidence, that 28 years later, I received an opportunity to write this chapter. I have known since I was a little girl that I was going to write a book. In fact, I have been writing a book for over seven years now. It's called *Rising Phoenix, Fallen Angel*. I saw this opportunity and the book title, along with the Phoenix on the cover. It grabbed my attention, immediately. Even more ironically, I am writing it in a home that belonged to my grandmother who passed away a few months ago. A woman I hardly knew, nor cared to know in the past.

The final fig leaf is letting go and letting God fully into my life. I can see the truth, generations of women in my family, who were lost, and sought their very essence in another human, usually MEN! Today, I am healing generational curses of motherless children, facing my own inadequacies or hypocrisies as a mother, and forgiving the women in my family who came before me. I know who they were now. They themselves had to grow up too soon and take care of everyone but themselves.

After 48 years of life, I can honestly say and KNOW and feel it to my very core. I finally know who Amanda really is. I am a woman who has been forged in fire, a warrior goddess. I love deeply, and I forgive quickly. I am a professional, and I carry myself with class. I am honest with myself and others, and I give more than I take. I have hurt people, and I have asked for forgiveness – and even if they did not forgive, I forgave myself. I live my life with integrity and give hope to those that need it.

I have sat with the broken, and I have dined with the rich. Money has never been my God, but it is nice to be able to provide financially to the monetary goals that I have for my future self. I am a WILD WOMEN, FORGED IN FIRE!, and I have risen from the ashes to become the warrior goddess that God has intended me to be all along.

# Forged in Fire

I am the wind in my hair, the sun on my face, the earth under my feet, and the water that flows through my body. I am connected to my source just for today. I choose to be awake and present, to participate in the life that God has given me.

If you feel lost and hear something inside your being, calling to you when you hear the words, "wild women and warrior goddess," maybe, just maybe, God brought you to read my story to help guide you on the path of creating your authentic self. I am not sure how to guide you in your journey or have all the answers to life's enigma on happiness. All I can offer is what helped me and what has continued to help me, staying true to myself but being compassionate to others. To always live with integrity, tell the truth, no matter the circumstance and the outcome. Staying connected to Source, God, Mother Mystery. To pay attention, and if things seem like they are falling apart, to be open to, maybe just maybe, they are actually falling together. To have an attitude of gratitude. To NOT BE SO DAMN SERIOUS, and to remember the little girl that loves to dance, sing in the shower, blow bubbles, to laugh until your stomach and face hurt, and to keep a childlike mentality. To pay attention to life's synchronicities, and to follow your bones and listen to your intuition.

I always know the answer. Sometimes it is simply hard to hear it or follow it. I do it kicking and screaming most of the time, because I THINK I KNOW (what a joke!). It is always easier to see the lessons looking backward, difficult to see them looking forward. Forgive, quickly, but make sure to protect your boundaries, and be an example for the younger women who are trying to "figure it out."

It is a wild ride, and I highly recommend finding who you are and being true to yourself, because in the end, you are all you have.

Affectionately, AFAYE!

# Amanda Faye Hartson

## About the Author

I am **Amanda F Hartson**. I am a native of northwest Arkansas, a realtor in Southern Tradition Real Estate, LLC, and I have a Bachelor of Science and a degree in Legal Studies.

I have three beautiful children, Ashlin Faye Elizabeth Hartson, Jey Jey Wayne Hartson, and Brian Lee Hartson, all of whom currently reside in southern Michigan. I also have three extraordinary grandchildren, Louis Keeley, Lukas Micheal, and Sylas Ray! I love nature, and enjoy any activity outdoors – golf, camp, canoe, fish, hunt, hike. You name it, I DO IT.

My monetary goals for my future self, is to travel, reside in Michigan with my kids during the summer months, and to be home with my immediate family in the winter months in Arkansas.

Family is important, and one day, we will all be together.

# Forged in Fire

# Find Me!

**LIVING AUTHENTICALLY** – Becoming the WILD WOMEN, the evolution of Phoenix to Wolf.

**AMANDA FAYE HARTSON** – a.k.a., AFAYE, Realtor
Southern Tradition Real Estate, LLC

https://www.facebook.com/amanda.f.hartson/

https://www.facebook.com/amandafayeSTRE

# How I Took Control of My Life Back From My Children

## Amber Stephenson
Confidence Coach, Canada

*"If you don't like your life, then change it."*
~ Amber Stephenson

### Crying on the Couch

Both of the babies were crying in the playpen, and I was sobbing on the couch. I was completely exhausted, and I couldn't handle the constant crying anymore.

The twins were 5 months old, and it had been a constant cycle of changing, feeding, and pumping. As soon as I finished with one baby, the other would wake up crying. I didn't have time to eat, sleep, or shower. I was exhausted and depressed. I was greasy, and I probably smelled. I can honestly say it was the worst time of my life.

I felt like I was a slave to my children, and no one had any good advice for me. All I kept hearing (when I was actually able to leave my house) was, "Oh, you must be so busy!" and a constant litany of *the kids come first*, even from my husband.

I hated every moment of my life because I was basically a slave to my two tiny children, and I even resented them for it. I yelled at them for being hungry and wanting comfort because, dammit!, I was hungry too!

I was so miserable that I called my husband, crying, at least three times a week to come home early so I could hide in the shower for a while and then maybe eat something.

I had developed severe post-partum depression, and finally, my husband convinced me to see my doctor and get medicated. It helped – a little. I only called him home once a week or so after that...

### Baby Steps

But it still wasn't enough. Nothing had actually changed in my life – the babies still cried in a constant cycle, one after the other, and I still didn't have time to take care of myself.

*The kids still came first!*

Even with my medication, I couldn't handle what my life had turned into. I needed to DO something about it, and I had an idea of what I could do.

I went on the Internet, and I started googling infant schedules. They'd been on a schedule in the NICU, so why not at home?

## Making a Decision

When my husband came home that night, I showed him the schedule I had created. I would feed the babies together every three hours with a slightly longer stretch at night. Then, they would sleep in the playpen next to me or in their crib while I showered.

He was furious! He said they were too young, that it wouldn't be good for them.

I looked him right in the eye, and I said, "This isn't good for ME! I am a shitty mom right now. How is that any better for them?"

He still disagreed, but since he wasn't at home during the day, I just went ahead with my plan... and you know what happened?

## The Light at the End of a Long, Dark Tunnel

The first morning I was able to eat a good breakfast, have a nice hot shower, AND wash the dishes – all before noon.

After a week, my husband grudgingly admitted that I had been right to make a schedule. I was smiling again. I had some (albeit limited) time to do things other than hold a bottle or change a diaper, the house was slowly getting somewhat cleaner, and I was calling him home less and less.

And this happened all because I decided that I was just as important as my kids.

Taking care of my basic needs made me a better mother. I wasn't yelling or crying anymore. I didn't feel like a slave or resent them for being needy. I got into a routine of making sure all of our needs were met – not just theirs.

# How I Took Control of My Life Back from My Children

## What I Want Every Mom to Know

Here's what I learned from my experience with post-partum depression:

1. Your children are NOT more important than you are. You are equally important and deserve just as much care and attention as they do.
2. No one knows what you need except you, and you have to be willing to ask for and/or take it for yourself.
3. You don't stop being an individual person when you become a mother. Your hopes, dreams, and ambitions don't disappear just because you created a human, and you shouldn't have to let go of them to be a "good mom."
4. People give really shitty advice – don't listen to it. Put a sign on your stroller, if you have to, but don't let people, especially complete strangers in Walmart, tell you how to live your life or raise your children.
5. If you want to change your circumstances, just do it. The worst that can happen is that you find something that doesn't work for you, but even then, you'll still be closer to a solution than you were before.

The twins are two and a half now, and half the time, they're holy terrors. (What two-year-old isn't, though?). My life looks so very different from where I was when I let them cry in the playpen. I wanted a way to bring more balance to my life, so I went and found it.

## Lifting Myself... and Others

I studied to become a Health and Life Coach and started a business, working from home with six-month-old twins. I started a mission to empower women everywhere to break out of the glass boxes society built for us and start living their dreams.

I want women everywhere to know that they deserve to live life on their own terms, do and be whatever their hearts desire, and break free of the expectation that women should be content to be mothers and not want anything outside of that.

I'm teaching this to all of my children. I hope that they'll pass it on to their children, and then their children and that I'll live to see the day when people really are allowed to decide on their own path in life – without judgment.

## Practical Advice to Help You Move Forward

1. Figure out what you want – and be specific.

## **Amber Stephenson**

    a. Do you want to have a career that you love? What will that career be?

    b. Do you want to stop worrying about how to pay your bills every month? How much money would allow you to do that? How can you create that amount of money?

2. Listen to your own inner voice. It will never steer you wrong, unlike people who haven't taken the time to understand your specific situation and struggles.

3. No one knows what you need better than you do, and sometimes you have to fight for it – even against your own family.

4. Get support. Doing things on your own is HARD! I did it that way in the beginning, and it was such a struggle. You need someone who can help identify what's holding you back and find ways to work through those roadblocks that actually work for your life. And the best person to do that is a Coach.

You CAN live the life you want.

*Amber Stephenson*

Amber Stephenson

You are a **Badass Goddess!**

# How I Took Control of My Life Back from My Children

## About the Author

**Amber Stephenson** is a Master Transformational Coach who specializes in helping women who struggle to reach their goals to identify what's holding them back and shift into success. She's on a mission to empower women to be their most powerful, authentic selves while building lives they love and making their dreams come true.

Amber is a Rockstar coach, a dedicated wife, mother of four, insatiable reader, and avid gamer.

# Amber Stephenson

# Find Me!

### Make Your Next 90 Days AMAZING:
https://mailchi.mp/c9ee95f7d66c/90amazingdays

### Need more Amber in your life?

**Send me a friend invite**: https://www.facebook.com/amber.kunde.3

**Connect on *LinkedIn***:
https://www.linkedin.com/in/amberstephensoncoach/

**Follow me on *Instagram***:
https://www.instagram.com/radiant_living_coaching/

**Send me an email**: radiantlivingcoach@gmail.com

# From Feeling Helpless to Owning My Life

## Catarina Rebelo
## Mom's Empowering Coach, Portugal

*"Use your hardest moments to say, 'That's Enough!'
and allow them to propel you forward."*
~ Catarina Rebelo

As I was coming home, I started screaming inside my car. I started crying, and I considered, for a brief moment, crashing my car into the road railing!

I should be ecstatic because I had left my daughter at school that morning, I had gone to work, and at that moment, I was going home for lunch to have some time for myself. So, why was I, a successful woman at her job with one lovely daughter and an amazing husband, screaming and crying in my car?

I was depressed. I was having anxiety attacks, and I was seeing a psychologist to help me deal with and cope with my life. When we were at home, I would scream with my daughter because I wasn't feeling good about myself. I took it out on her, or I would resent my husband and snap at him because we were always having trouble paying our bills.

I felt that it wasn't fair that I was in that situation, that all the money I had saved before our marriage had all been spent. I couldn't figure out a way to make more money besides the money coming in from our jobs. I had to keep asking for help from my parents, and I felt I didn't deserve the money they gave me. I would snap at my mom when all that she wanted was love, but I couldn't show her that because I was ashamed of not being able to pay for my bills.

## Catarina Rebelo

I believed that we could do anything we want in life, so why couldn't I? I felt like I was dying inside but kept a straight and happy face for the world to see.

I finally reached a moment in time when I said to myself, *That's enough! I can't keep on doing this!* I didn't want to be in pain anymore. I started watching myself from the outside shouting at my daughter and being detached from my husband. I decided I had enough of that.

I had just started my Coaching journey and wanted to achieve my life goals; that's when I decided I would do just that. Suddenly, I could see myself as an accomplished Coach, travelling the world with my family and speaking at events. That had never happened before.

Before then, I would try to see what I wanted, and I always saw myself as I was at that moment, doing the same things over and over again.

**So, What Changed?**

I finally realized that what changed was that I started believing in myself. I forgave myself for procrastinating, for being where I was in my life and not where I wanted to be, and that's when I started moving forward.

At that moment, I decided I had to keep growing. So I went after my Coaching Certification, which I finished in April 2019. At that time, I was pregnant with my second daughter, and when she was born on June 1st, I was delighted and decided to enjoy those few first months at home with her.

I had recently met a Life Coach, and I felt I needed help to move forward, so I hired her. That's when I began the journey of finding myself, finding my values, breaking limiting beliefs, and enjoying life again with my family. It took me a while, but I got there, and afterward, I kept going and decided that my professional life was coming to the 20-year mark, and I just didn't want it anymore.

I loved my boss, colleagues, and all the friends I had made throughout the years. However, that wasn't for me anymore. So, I hired a Business Coach, and I went after my passion.

I have always wanted to build my own business and be the master of my time and earn enough money to help my family thrive. By doing this, I would also be showing my kids that anything is possible if they put their heart and mind into it and take massive, imperfect action. And, most importantly, enjoy the process, enjoy the journey.

# From Feeling Helpless to Owning My Life

## I Grew Up in a Society Where Women Were Expected to Do Everything

They were expected to take care of their home, take care of their kids, take care of their husbands, and take care of people who depend on them, like my grandmother. I was taught to always say yes to everything people asked of me – and I forgot to take care of myself; I forgot that I am the most important person in my life. I was taught that thinking about myself was egotistical. So, I felt guilty when I took time for myself and never enjoyed it fully.

I always wanted more for myself and my family, but I always felt unworthy of it. So, I sabotaged myself. I wouldn't put all my effort behind every endeavor I took. I never went all in. I would only dabble and never saw any meaningful results. That would only confirm my mother's suspicions that I was unable to do certain things, and I felt she was right. That would kill me inside. But how could she believe in me if I didn't believe in myself?

So, when I met a Life Coach, it seemed the right time to move forward with my life and leave my depression behind me. I decided then and there I would stop the psychologist sessions and immerse myself in my get better process with my coach and newfound strength. To say that I had suddenly got better and accomplished my dreams would be lying. It was a difficult process of going back and forward. I would walk two steps forward and fall one behind, over and over again, but I started seeing results. They were slim at first, but quickly started coming with more and more frequency.

A certainty that I would be alright began to grow inside of me, and slowly, I became that cheerful person I was before, always smiling and laughing, full of life. I began enjoying the time I spent with my kids as well as the time spent with my husband and I started to believe in new possibilities, I began seeing new opportunities and really living my life again and not just surviving.

It's amazing how we moms wear so many different hats. We are moms, wives, daughters, and granddaughters. We hold our homes together; we have a job and sometimes have a side business. With so many things going on, it would be normal to ask for help, but so many times, we feel we can and should be able to do everything ourselves and asking for help never comes to mind.

So many times, we find ourselves in over our heads. We feel we are not enough and start doubting ourselves. We become anxious and sometimes even depressed, and the answer could be as simple as asking for help from our family or friends. They want us to be happy, they want to help, but they don't know how and often, we don't appreciate them when they do help. Something I craved was time for myself, and I felt egotistical of not wanting to spend every waking moment with my family.

When I decided to finally begin the journey of healing myself and going after what I wanted and not just what other people thought was best for me, I finally realized I had so much more to offer. I already wore so many hats! I could enjoy wearing them all, asking for help when I needed it. I could even stop doing things I did not enjoy and not feel guilty about it, like household duties. I decided to focus on doing the things I enjoyed and ask for help or even hire someone to do the others. My husband helps me a lot at home, and I started acknowledging that. He is an amazing husband and father, devoted to our children and me.

When I come to think of it, time is money, and I am willing to spend money on things I am not particularly happy doing so I can have more time doing what I really love, like spending time with my family and being of service to those who can be helped with the knowledge I gained in this process.

This realization made me a better mom, wife, daughter, granddaughter, worker, and friend because I started to enjoy my life and my business as I had never done before. When we start moving towards our vision, every area of our life improves.

I have learnt that by waking up early, I start the day in a better mood, happier and fulfilled. It allows me to set an intention for how I want the rest of the day to go by. I choose to be present and happy, and I feel I have already accomplished something important for myself. The day goes by much more smoothly, and even if I am not able to accomplish anything else that day, I am already happy with what I did that morning.

No matter where you are in your life right now, I have found that my past is what allowed me to learn a few lessons necessary to bring me to where I am today. These are the lessons I have learned:

**Lesson 1: Accept & Forgive Yourself**

For a long time, I could not accept the fact that I can't do everything myself, that I had to be okay with accepting help from others and accept my life as it was at that moment. I also blamed myself for not being able to do more but also for not earning more money so we could have a better life and accomplish our dreams of travelling around the world, of building a sustainable home with a backyard, an organic vegetable garden, and fruit trees, or simply just not being able to eat out more often or order in.

It was only when I forgave myself for not being a superwoman, but a woman with a beautiful, loving family, an amazing apartment, and a full-time job that I actually liked, was I able to move forward and finally began taking action to accomplish my dreams.

That's when I realized I had so much to offer.

## Lesson 2: Get Out of your Head/Enjoy your Journey

For a long time, I would get anxious and nervous about paying the bills and wanted to earn more money. I would forget to enjoy the day and enjoy the time spent with my children. I would be living in my head instead of living my life.

It was only when I realized that I already had so much of what I dreamed of having and when I started to be grateful for what I already achieved that I started to enjoy the present and live my life completely.

I knew I wanted more and worked consistently towards those goals while I enjoyed every moment fully. To say that it all happened in an instant would be an understatement. This was a process I went through slowly with ups and downs, but I became stronger and stronger as time went by.

## Lesson 3: Give Back

For most of my life, I was a saver. I saved all the money I could only to spend it in an instant on something I wanted, like an online course. Only recently did I realize that I love learning new things when it comes to personal development. Still, for the longest time, I would buy these courses and not make the most out of them. I would be wasting my money, and I ended up feeling bad because I had wasted all the money I earned and saved so diligently.

So, it was only when I became aware of this pattern of behavior and came to terms with this that I was able to enjoy what money could bring. I realized that the most important thing I could do with it was actually helping others who needed it more than I did, like my grandmother and Mother Earth by helping to reforest the planet. That's also when I decided that it was my mission to show other moms just like me that they had so much potential and so much to offer that they could build their own dream life and accomplish their deepest desires if that's what they truly wish.

# Catarina Rebelo

## Lesson 4: Surround Yourself with Amazing People

When I started on my Coaching journey, I became connected with so many extraordinary people online and offline. I have learned so much from them on my way to becoming who I am as a person and as a Coach.

Make sure you are always surrounded by people that are at least a step ahead of you because they will then show you what it is possible. Become aware of what you can learn from them, what their habits and behaviours are you can adopt for yourself. These will help you get what you want.

## Lesson 5: Focus Only on the Next Step

This was the hardest lesson I had to learn. I had the bad habit of wanting to do many things at once because I was never a patient person. My mind is always full of ideas. So, I had to learn to become patient and focus only on the next step I had to take.

Sometimes, I still fall into this trap of thinking I can do many things at the same time. However, what always happens is that I end up doing nothing at all. This leaves me drained, and I fall into the procrastination trap, which leads to feeling overwhelmed and anxious. By focusing on one goal at a time and getting it done, I get a feeling of accomplishment and gratefulness that allows me to be fully present in the moment, enjoy my journey and celebrate my wins.

What do you want? What fulfils you? Go for it and start living Your Amazing Life!

The lessons I learned on my journey from feeling helpless to owning my life have made me stronger and have allowed me to become a better version of myself, evolving every day and giving back to the world.

On this journey, I have come to realize that I want to help moms who want to live their dream life by becoming the best version of themselves. For that reason, I have developed my signature program, **Empowering Moms to Own their Life!**

I help them get clarity on who they are and what they want, and why. They become confident, accept that they are enough and take action on their goals by focusing on what matters, enjoying their journey, and celebrating their wins.

I have seen hundreds of women take action towards their goals, become fulfilled, and enjoy their motherhood at the same time. I know that in the end, it all comes down to believing in ourselves and taking one step

# From Feeling Helpless to Owning My Life

at a time.

I am enjoying my life deeply again while raising two children under seven years old, still working full time, and being the best Coach and entrepreneur I can be.

I deeply believe that **You Can Too**!

## Takeaways

So, to recap some key takeaways from this chapter:

1. Fill in the blank: I need to _____ myself to move forward and take action.
2. Who should I surround myself with?
3. Don't try doing everything at the same time. What should you focus on instead?

## Action Steps

Here are three action steps you can take to help you with a breakthrough in your life:

1. **Know What You Want!** What do you want to accomplish? What is your purpose/mission in life? What do you like to do? What do you value? Who do you want to help? Brainstorm your ideas and dream big. **Take Action!**
2. **Set a Daily Intention!** How do you want to live your life? What actions do you choose to take to live your life on your own terms? What habits and behaviours do you want to change? Visualize yourself living your life the way you want to. **Take Action!**
3. **Invest in Your Growth!** Have you tried to make changes by yourself only to give up after a few days? Do you find yourself procrastinating, lacking clarity or confidence? Investing in ourselves sends a signal to our subconscious that says, "I am ready!" It also helps make faster transformations and avoiding costly mistakes. Suddenly, it all becomes possible. **Take Action!**

*"Find out what fulfils you, take action, and see your whole life improve."*

## Catarina Rebelo

My friend, you are amazing!

Catarina Rebelo

# From Feeling Helpless to Owning My Life

## About the Author

My name is **Catarina Rebelo**, I am from Lisbon, Portugal, and I am passionate about helping moms realize they have so much to be grateful for and that they can be and have all that they want. I am on a mission to **Empower Moms to Own their Life!**

I'm married to John, a wonderful Colombian man. I am the mother of two beautiful girls (two and eight years old), and I help moms who want **Clarity and Confidence** to **Take Massive Action** by empowering themselves to own their journey.

I am usually dressed comfortably in jeans and a blouse, and I love reading inspiring books and playing with my kids at the park as well as dancing salsa and going to the movies with my husband.

It is my pleasure to help you on your journey towards your dream life while enjoying every moment of it.

**You are amazing!**
**You are deserving!**
**You are enough!**

# Catarina Rebelo

# Find Me!

### Empowering Moms to Own their Life!

**Download your Free Gift:** http://www.catarinarebelocoach.com/gifts

*Facebook*: https://www.facebook.com/catarinafrebelo/

*LinkedIn:* https://www.linkedin.com/in/catarina-rebelo/

*Instagram:* https://www.instagram.com/catarinarebelocoach/

**Email:** catarinarebelocoach@gmail.com

# A Journey to Me

## Erika Olson
## Spiritual Life Coach, USA

*"Mysterious ways! I am grateful for the path that has led me on. Trusting in my connection to spirit and God have led me to the greatest life I could life!"*
~ Erika Olson

In the spring of 2018, I found myself on the side of the road, sobbing. I had worked myself into a tizzy about going to a doctor's appointment, to which I arrived late. When they said the doctor couldn't see me, I lost my mind. I sobbed with the receptionist as she jumped through hoops to get me into someone else as soon as possible. She was kind and gentle and was genuinely concerned. She assured me that I was okay, asking if I wanted her to call my husband. I quietly said no and gathered my wits, knowing that I could get help the next day. My prayer was that the doctor would give me a pill to make everything better.

While I was driving home, my husband called me. He was concerned because I had been gone much longer than I should have been. I realized that not only had I been driving for about 20 minutes, but I was lost. I pulled over and waited for my husband to find me. Thank goodness for an app that we both had on our phones since we first started seeing each other that enabled us to locate each other. Winters in Wisconsin can be tough.

At the appointment the next day, I was told that I had "Generalized Anxiety" and that I should change my eating habits. I was overweight and was taking Xanax®. I was numb. The doctor told me that he wasn't surprised that I was experiencing anxiety due to my other health concerns. No reason other than that. No helpful tips or even ways to live with it except another medication. That's what I wanted, though, right? I blindly filled the prescription and began what I thought was the beginning of my middle mid-life crisis.

This was the beginning of the end, but not how you may think...

# Erika Olson

My husband was supportive and encouraging when we discussed what I wanted to do with my career. I had been working in a call center for the past ten years. I decided to go back to what I loved. In 2016, I began a journey that has been one hell of a trip. I decided to return to a career that I loved after allowing my body to recover from an injury. I went back to school to get my Associate Degree in Massage Therapy.

I was blessed to work for a woman who saw a spark in me and was willing to nurture it. Bodywork lit up my soul. I began to incorporate Reiki energy work into my treatments and my life. My schedule at work as a massage therapist grew, and I started to be booked out for four to six weeks in advance. I worked my way up to managing the spa, and it is here where my true "midlife crisis" happened.

In my research on how to help myself and my clients, I found energy work to be very helpful. I was able to use Reiki energy to be a conduit with my guests' energy and allow them to heal. I heard comments about how relaxed they felt, how much lighter their spirit was. Many of them came back and told me that they had experienced breakthroughs in their own life, particularly where they had been at a standstill.

I was curious as to how I could continue this with my clients and ease the pressure on my physical body. I don't exactly know where the thought to be a Life Coach came from, but it was a strong thought indeed. I knew that I had always had "extra gifts," as my grandma would say. I was around the age of three when I talked to my mom and grandma about the lady in the rocking chair. My highly sensitive personality allowed me to connect with others in a way that most didn't. I was told by friends, clients, and coworkers that I was a gifted intuitive. I knew things that they couldn't figure out how I knew. I began to meditate more, search out coaches, and try to find ways to push and elevate my own life. I also deepened my faith in order to help make sense of everything.

I had been a child of divorce with my fair share of trouble, but I understood that I was very blessed. God had put many situations and people in front of me to make sure that I got to the path of coaching. I have heard from past employees who still reach out to thank me for listening and giving them advice – that they still follow – and from current employees I am honored to coach through their own business and life situations.

The true turning point of becoming a coach happened on two distinct occasions. The first was the day that I was deciding to actually sign up to attend a Coaching school where I would become a Spiritual Life Coach. I had been researching many programs, spending many hours weighing pros and cons and what-ifs. I finally did the most solid thing one could do – I left it up to chance! I decided that if I had made more than $50 in tips that day, I would sign up for school. I made $52.

The second was a true confirmation. I was with my stepmother in Israel, and this trip would prove to be life-changing for me in many ways. My

## A Journey to Me

connection with God has been turbulent, to say the least. The moment I want to share with you was when I was at the Sea of Galilee. We were at Tabgha where, in the Bible, Jesus fed 4,000 people with just seven loaves of bread and fish. I could feel the water lapping at my feet and was gazing out over the water. The pastor from our group came up to me and said, "You know He is there, and the answer is yes." He put his arm around me and gave me a squeeze and the most gentle smile.

I was stunned! How could he have known what I was contemplating? He said yes – yes to me becoming a coach, and yes to me believing in my own abilities. He said yes to the gift of intuitive guidance. At that moment, I knew that God had made me be a voice for others, a person who stands and holds space for people with big dreams. God had given me a yes.

What I did next will shock and amaze you!

I DID NOTHING! I was changed from the trip but still questioned everything. I was deep into an autoimmune disease flare-up and in immense physical pain. I was back to wallowing in my own misery, blaming everything and everyone else. I was scared to be psychic because of what everyone else would think. I was ashamed to talk to others about how they could improve their lives when my own life was a mess. How could I coach others when I didn't have my life together?

The answer to that came while I was in my pajamas, having a movie day, while my husband worked. I was reminded to make "small moves." I knew that if I didn't make some changes I would never grow.

Change and moving forward meant changing my thoughts. Negative, hurtful thoughts and the "mean girl" on my shoulder had been with me all along, and I was miserable. My thoughts were the things that I could change and see almost immediate results. This isn't magic. It takes is work. I found that while I thought I was ruled by my emotions, the reality was that I *let* my emotions rule me and my decisions. Each day I make the decision to change my thoughts from negative to positive. Thanks to this, I have changed how I respond to certain triggers. It is a lot of good, hard work.

Thanks to that daily determination, I am able to be calm and more joyful. It is a choice I *get* to make. There are days that I choose to be grumpy and tired or even lazy, but the beauty is that those are okay, too. I now see that there is no "bad" emotion. I no longer have to be the "good girl." I get to be me. In all my loudness, emotions are fully expressed. It isn't perfect, but it is worth the work.

This is the gift I want to share with the world. I am an intuitive Spiritual Life Coach, and that means that I get to stand with you as you make changes in your core thoughts, beliefs, and life. I work with women who have been or are at their own personal rock bottom; women who know there is more to life than where they are now; women who know they have gifts but are fearful to use them or are even unsure how to use them; women to connect with

## Erika Olson

something or someone bigger than themselves; and most of all, women who want to change!

What I have learned through this experience is that change is good. I still take medication if the anxiety is beyond my mental ability to control, but I no longer rely on it to keep me grounded in the here and now. If I don't like the mood I am in or the situation I am in, I know that I can always change it.

I am blessed to see these changes in my friends, family, and clients. I simply adore seeing women believe in their big dreams. I am living my God-driven, universe-supported Big Dream!

*Erika Olson*

# A Journey to Me

## About the Author

**Erika Olson** is a Certified Spiritual Life Coach and an intuitive (psychic medium), licensed massage therapist and Usui Reiki Master.

She lives in Wisconsin with her husband Jeff, her step daughter, Anika and their goldendoodle, Rocky. Erika is an avid camper, she loves cooking and gardening. Erika opened Intuitive Grace where she can use her intuitive gifts to coach, giving readings, and work as a spiritual mentor. She sees clients remotely and in person for those who are close enough.

Erika is a licensed massage therapist and Reiki Master. She truly enjoys continuing to serve people and witness them heal themselves. Through Intuitive Grace, she helps women who are ready to say yes to themselves to overcome their fears, create a growth- and abundant-mindset, and embrace their true self while embracing all the messiness.

# Erika Olson

## Find Me!

*Facebook:* https://www.facebook.com/IntuitiveGraceErika

*Instagram:* https://www.instagram.com/intuitivegrace.erika/

*TikTok:* https://www.tiktok.com/@intuitivegrace

**Website:** www.intuitivegrace.net

**Email:** Erika@IntuitiveGrace.net

# The New You

## Dr. Izdihar Jamil, Ph.D.
## Business Coach, USA

*"When things become heavy, put in a pause. It's time for a change. It's time for a NEW YOU to arise!"*
~Dr. Izdihar Jamil, Ph.D.

## The Unexpected

Two blue lines... *It's a positive! I'm pregnant! I can't believe it. After seven years, God gave us a miracle.* I told my husband, and he was shocked. I thought our time had passed. *But how could it be? Could this really be happening to us after all this time?* Our doctor confirmed our results from my blood test. Yes, we are going to be having our third child. *Our miracle baby!*

Suddenly, I felt a wave of panic. I had finally found my freedom – no more nursing, late-night feeding, and nappy changing. For the last two years, I could travel to retreats and business events without my children as my kids are older and more independent. Since 2018, I set myself a goal of having a "ME time" without the kids, and I have been fulfilling those goals every year. Until now...

My life and business were about to be disrupted with a newborn. It's like going back to basics, and I'm scared. I've worked hard to build my coaching and consultancy business for the last two years. *What if I lost everything? What if I lose my clients because I have to take time out when the baby comes? How am I going to manage a baby, two kids, and a business together?* I can't breathe.

Yes, I feel beyond grateful for the miracle, and yet I'm scared at the same time. I know it doesn't make sense. People told me that everything is going to be fine. *But how?* I knew my life and business was going to change. So, I have started to put down a new structure in my business to prepare for the birth.

My vision was that when the baby comes, the business can run without me. That's what the experts said: *Build a system and a team so that the business can run without you,* or, *A true business is when you can walk away, and it still makes money for you.* I'm beginning to realize that those perspectives are a bunch of "fluff." The so-called experts are men. How would they know what pregnancy or nursing or nighttime feeding looks like? They are not the ones who have to deal with all that. We do – the women.

I'm still missing something. I don't know what. *Will I ever find it? Will I truly be able to run my business while looking after a baby and two kids?* I'm uncertain, and it's killing me.

## The Birth

I woke up at 2 a.m. and felt something was off. I went to the bathroom and saw that I had some blood discharge. I sent a message to my midwife and doula, who confirmed that I'm at the early stage of labor. But how can it be? I'm not ready yet. There are a million things that I haven't done for my business yet. I haven't even prepared the baby bag, and now I'm having early labor?

The thing is, within a few hours, I've got three sales calls scheduled. One side of me wanted to continue with the calls despite my contractions. *You can do it. You just need to show up. You shouldn't be breaking your promise. It's not good for your business!* a little voice inside me said. Then the other side of me said, *You need to stop. The baby is coming. You need to get ready. You're having contractions. You need to focus on you!* Which one should I listen to?

In the end, I let go of "looking good" and informed my potential clients that I'm having early labor and would need to reschedule my calls. I could feel a breathing space, a space where I can focus on myself and my baby. We are finally going to meet him!

At 9 p.m., my water broke, and my midwife told me to come to the birth center to prepare for the baby. I arrived at 10 p.m. and went through the routine checks and preparation. I have opted for an easy and nurturing water birth, something that I had always wanted. I had a fabulous team of midwives and a doula who supported me.

I remembered one of the midwives asked me, "How long do you think it will be before the baby will come? Four hours?"

I said, *No, in one hour. I can't stand it anymore!*

And true enough, my little one came in less than an hour. My birth was powerful, and my hope for an easy, nurturing, water birth was materialized. I was in bliss. At that time, nothing else mattered except my baby and me.

## The Breakdown

When I returned home, I felt it was my re-birth. I had to learn to breastfeed my baby. In the beginning, it was painful. If you have nursed your child before, you know it isn't easy. The constant feeding and the thought of having a little one so dependent on you can be overwhelming. I was tired and exhausted. I barely slept.

I'm really grateful that my husband took a few weeks off to support me. He became my rock and looked after our two other kids and did all the housework. My friends created a meal plan and cooked for my family and me for two weeks. That's one huge burden that was lifted, and I'm so thankful that

# The New You

I have amazing friends.

I'm learning to become a mom to a newborn again. Everything is new – nappy change, nighttime feeding, nursing, doubting myself that I'm doing a good job. But as the days passed, I became more confident with myself. Things started to flow, and I could feel myself healing.

I've delegated my work to my team. I stopped checking my emails. I stopped checking my social media. A part of me knew that things are going to be okay even if I was not there, but one part of me was scared, too. What if I'm left with a huge mess with my business?

When I did check my emails, I was bombarded with things that needed to be done. How can this be? I thought I've taken care of things before the baby came. I felt like there was this huge mountain that seemed impossible for me to conquer. The last thing I wanted is having to deal with business stuff while caring for a newborn.

## The Rise

I knew at that moment that I needed to shift. The things that I've done in the past weren't working anymore. I'm a mom of three now. I have three kids, including a newborn, and I'm running my business at the same time. It is time for a NEW ME to arise.

During my 44-day confinement period, I created that space for me to heal. That was a sacred moment. My health and my newborn baby were a priority. I took some time to breathe.

With my business, I trusted my team to handle things. Even if things don't go my way, I trust that it's going to work out.

*One Communication Method*

I've simplified my communication methods and use only email as the communication method between my clients and me. I only respond to emails that are critical and let the rest go. Gone are the days when I'm using multiple social media platforms (*Facebook*, *LinkedIn*, *Instagram*, *Twitter*) to communicate with my clients. It doesn't work for me to overstretch myself. I chose one method – email and nothing else. That means email is my priority, and the rest is just "noise."

*Boundaries*

I informed potential clients that I was not accepting any calls due to my maternity leave. At first, I was scared that I was going to lose opportunities, but I trusted that what is meant for me will never miss me, and what misses me was never meant for me. It's okay to put a pause on things.

*Responsibility Shift*

Rather than you taking the responsibility of coaching your clients, think about how you can empower them. That means rather than giving you, you give them a proven system to help them get the results. In other words, you shift the responsibility over to them. Your time is expensive. It's sacred. Your clients are adults. They can handle it.

For example, with my book clients, I would give them a writing formula, an online course, and a planner so that they could be responsible for taking action on completing their books. With my magazine, I inform my contributors that they need to have their articles proofread before submission. For my media clients, I would outsource the copywriting to my team rather than doing it myself.

*Collaboration*

Look for collaboration within your network to get the same results while taking one thing less from your plate. For example, with my multi-author book projects, I found an agency doing the same thing and collaborating with other entrepreneurs. That means rather than having to do it all myself, I could include my clients in their book projects. This means there's less pressure for me to perform and do all the work.

Another new collaboration that came up is for my clients to get featured in high-profile media such as *Forbes, Entrepreneurs, Business Insiders, Oprah,* and many more. A senior *Forbes* writer reached out to me to collaborate by providing her expertise to guide female entrepreneurs with her intimate knowledge about the media and for me to extend the invitation to my trusted circle. This way, I have outsourced the training part to another expert while I concentrate on converting clients.

*New Business Model*

I asked for support. My amazing coach, Carly Hope, was there for me. I shared with her my challenges – I can't do a back-to-back sales and coaching calls any more with a baby. I don't feel comfortable nursing while talking to clients and potential clients. I feel scared to book any calls because my baby's routine is unpredictable, and I don't like to cancel as it impacts my credibility.

Here are some ideas that Carly and I have hashed out to fit my new lifestyle:

- **New Sales Methods.** Rather than me going on 1:1 sales calls, I would implement a structure using various media to close a sale. For example, when interests come in, I would send them a questionnaire to understand their needs and see if they are a good fit. Then, I would send them a pre-recorded video/training session and convert them from there.

- **Get to choose.** I can't work with everybody. I don't want to work with just anybody, and it's okay to let go of those who aren't ready.

# The New You

- **Build a Sales Team**. Hire a team member that will handle sales for me. Preferably, it will be someone who is experienced in sales, believes in my products, and are aligned with my principles and values.

- **Click and Buy.** Master a "Click-and-Buy" Sales Page conversion. So, after attracting the leads, qualifying them, and warming them up via video and emails, I would send them to a "Click-and-Buy" sales page.

- **Pre-qualify.** Before proceeding on any business ventures, it's best for you to pre-qualify potential clients to see if they are really serious about moving forward. You can do this by creating a simple questionnaire. Remember, your time is precious and sacred. Not everybody deserves it.

*Abundance*

I trusted that my provision is secured, that God will take care of my family and me, and true enough, an abundance of opportunities came my way. I had multiple requests from new clients that reached out to me. I have been invited to become a guest speaker at various international events. I've been approached by leaders and influencers from the industry collaborate with them. My existing clients wanted to do a new project with me.

## The Lessons

Having a baby is a circuit breaker. I feel that God is gifting me with this miracle so that I could ascend to a new Me, to the one who truly lives by her core – FREEDOM in all aspects of my life and business. Otherwise, I would still be tied to the "traditional" way of running my business. More importantly, it is finding a feminine business model that works for my business and family life that was not created by male experts who may not know what it's like to have babies while running a business.

Here are my lessons for any women who have been forced to make a big lifestyle change, and how you can use it as an opportunity to elevate:

- **Simplify.** Simplify your life and business. If you could only do one thing all day, every day, what would it be? For example, I've chosen email as my #1 tool of communication. The rest are just "noise," and I could let them go.

- **Sales 2.0**. If you can't be there for sales calls, how can you make money? This is your opportunity to be creative. For example, you can learn to master video-based conversions or nail down an email sequence that leads to conversion.

## Dr. Izdihar Jamil, Ph.D.

- **Build a team.** If possible, build it with someone with experience so that you don't have to spend a lot of time and money training them. Your team can include a virtual assistance, bookkeeper, and salesperson – or anyone that you need to grow your business so you can focus on what matters.

- **Trust.** Trust that your provision is secured for you by the Creator. Trust that He will never leave you. Trust that the best clients and team members will come your way. Trust your heart in guiding you even when things are scary.

- **Opportunities.** When you start to let go of things, you'll see that there is an abundance of opportunities coming your way. Some are already in front of you, but you didn't see them. By being open and creative, I found how I can get the same results in my business while doing less – for example, by collaborating with other agencies or entrepreneurs.

- **Sacred time.** Remember, your time is sacred and precious. Not everybody deserves it. If they are not ready, put them on your list so you can have touchpoints via email with them over a period of time. Trust that when they're ready, they'll reach out to you.

- **Collaboration.** Look within your industry. Be open and set your intentions to ask for experts who can help you get the same results and take one more thing off your plate.

## Power Summary

Let's summarize the key points in this chapter:

- Name one idea that I have mentioned that I used to help me rise from my challenges.
- What is one new sales method that I used to be free from 1:1 calls?
- If you could do one thing in your business, what would you do every day, all day? What is your answer?
- Fill in the blank. Rather than giving them you, you would give them a _____ to help them get the results.

## Key Actions

- What is one method that you can implement to be free from 1:1 sales and grow your business?

## The New You

- Name one person in your industry that you can collaborate with to help you get the same results with minimal effort.
- What is one thing that you can do to simplify your life and business? Example: Use only emails as your form of communications from now on.

> *"Trust that God will take care of your provision. What is meant for your will never miss you. What misses you was never meant for you!"*
> ~ Dr. Izdihar Jamil

Love and blessings,

Izdihar

# Dr. Izdihar Jamil, Ph.D.

## About the Author

**Dr. Izdihar Jamil, Ph.D.**, is a computer scientist turned business owner. She is an immigrant, hijab-wearing Muslim woman running a successful business in America despite coming from a marginalized community with English as her second language. She is an influential trailblazer and an inspiring leader in helping female entrepreneurs be the #1 Go-To Expert in their fields. She's a #1 Bestselling Author of *It Is Done!* and was featured on *Forbes*, *Fox TV*, and *TED-Ed*.

In September 2020, she was chosen to be on the front cover of *The Corporate Escapist* magazine because of her inspirational story. In June 2021, she appeared on the front cover of *The Spotlight Entrepreneur* magazine for becoming an influential trailblazer in her industry.

It is her greatest pleasure to see women having confidence in themselves and be successful in their business so they can have the best of both worlds. Her methods are proven, simple, and effective – designed to produce the fastest results possible for her clients.

Izdihar lives in California with her husband and children. In her spare time, she loves reading and baking for her family.

# The New You

## Find Me!

**Website**: www.izdiharjamil.com

**Email**: hello@izdiharjamil.com

**Facebook**: https://www.facebook.com/izdihar.jamil.1

**Instagram**: https://www.instagram.com/izdiharjamil/

**LinkedIn**: https://www.linkedin.com/in/izdihar-jamil-ph-d-97236598/

**Twitter**: @IzdiharJamil

**FREE Gift: The Fast Authority Accelerator Scholarship**
https://www.izdiharjamil.com/fast-authority

# Dare Not to Neglect Thyself

## LaMeshia Conley
## Content Strategist Coach, USA

*"Authenticity is the alignment of head, mouth, heart, and feet – thinking, saying, feeling, and doing the same thing – consistently. This builds trust and followers love leaders they can trust."*
~ Lance Secretan

## Peeling Away My Pseudo-Self

As soon as the car stopped, I got out in the middle of traffic, left the whole family in the car, crossed a huge intersection, and began walking by myself until the sidewalk ended. I crossed a freeway bridge and saw a farmers' market ahead, and I went at least a half-mile before a colleague saw me walking and asked me to get in the car. I was so furious, I literally could have walked until I couldn't physically walk anymore, but she was adamant, so I got in the car.

Now the Moment of Truth had come. I had to tell the truth about why I was walking across a freeway bridge. Of course, an overwhelming amount of embarrassment came over me because in her eyes, I was a fantastic woman. In her eyes, I was Superwoman because I was handling my business as a mom, as a wife, and as a woman with multiple businesses. Ultimately, I didn't want to fail her or taint her image of me, but I just had to keep it real.

What's crazy is she didn't really ask me any personal questions. She did ask me if I was going home, and I said no. She asked how was II was feeling, and I told her I was not good. I had my head down the whole time, and then she asked if I wanted something to eat. She said she was heading home, and I could come over and relax. I agreed, so we stopped for food and went to her home.

All during this time, another colleague was trying to reach me on my phone, but I refused to pick up. I really did not know how to express what I was feeling, but I knew that I had to get what I was feeling out. In our time in the car, I realized I can be freely me, and I didn't have to hide who I was. She was so open to understanding who I really was, and I was eager to show her and

# LaMeshia Conley

tell her.

When we got to her house, she said, "Make yourself at home. Here's the bathroom, and you can use this remote to watch whatever you want." So, I turned my phone off and binge-watched *Moesha*, *The Parkers*, and *The Game* for the rest of the day.

Hours before that morning, we were just on a business conference call to help us become better leaders to serve our customers. I presented myself as a leader who shows up and does everything they're supposed to do. And then, there I was, walking across the bridge by myself, angry, disgusted, sad, and emotional to the point that I can't even express my emotions fully because they're all mixed and bottled up together. When my colleague picked me up, she didn't need to ask me any questions because she knew that I knew that something was going on. She knew that whenever I was ready to share, then I would share.

I knew this is not who I am. I knew that I was made for greater than how I was now acting out to be. I really just didn't know how to be myself because for a long time, I had been inauthentic and a people-pleaser. Then, all the while on the inside, I was really losing the inner battle with myself. I was an angry mom. I was a silent wife. I was just trying to show up as a great, positive businesswoman and CEO, but I was not even hitting my goals in my business because the other areas of life were failing as well.

I stopped taking care of myself and everyone else around me.

## The Start

Let me tell you when this all started...

This all started when I had graduated from college, and I could not get my dream job. I mean, first of all, it's a great accomplishment to graduate with a bachelor's degree, or so the world says, but after college, I worked at a gas station, a home health center, and I worked at a call center before I decided to go and get my master's degree. I was under the impression that you could make more money if you get a master's degree.

My main goal was to make enough money to travel before any of my kids came. So, I got my master's degree at Full Sail University. It was great. I loved the experience. After college, I did not get my dream job that ultimately was supposed to help me pay off the student loans that I had to get to attend college. So, here I am, with two degrees and less money than I had before I started college!

By this time, I knew more than enough to land my dream job, and I had the work ethic to compete – but I never got it. I used headhunters and I used all types of third-party resources. I even used school resources so that I could create the right resume. By this time, because of my multiple skillsets, I had three different resumes that I could use to apply for three type different types of positions. I even got a separate email address just to send my resume from.

# Dare Not to Neglect Thyself

I never found or I never landed my dream job, and I continued to work menial customer service jobs anything that was easy, because I still have hf bills that I needed to pay.

At that time, I felt like if I was going to work a job, then I needed to do something I liked to do, like working with youth and toddlers. So one year, I worked at a daycare center with two- and three-year-olds. In another year, I worked in the school system as a substitute teacher so I could stay connected with my teaching gift. I did not want to become a full-time teacher because that would require a whole new degree, and I wasn't pulling out anymore student loans.

I joined a few network marketing companies just for extra money and also for the product perks. At one point, I worked five part-time jobs at once just so that I can have some sort of identity with what I went to school for. It was like a closure for me because I wanted to feel accomplished. It wasn't enough to graduate with two degrees and possibly go to school again just to get another degree to feel accomplished. I wanted to land a dream job so that I could feel more accomplished. Instead, my choices ended up having me work five different part-time jobs just so that I could feel fulfilled on a career end.

Realizing that wasn't going to work in what I initially wanted, I decided to combine all that I knew about communication, social media marketing, public relations, and videography and use those skills to freelance and keep one job. I felt more accomplished freelancing for local small business owners and keeping a part-time job for supplemental income. All the while, I was trying to feel more accomplished within myself, but I was losing an outer battle. I was involved in an unhealthy marriage, and then the kids showed up. I lived in only what was a potential instead of what could have been a reality. I wanted a certain lifestyle for my kids, but I had not created it before they came. I wanted so much more than what I had, and I couldn't figure out how to get there. So, while trying to escape this inauthentic life I created, I didn't want my kids to see the inauthenticity or do what I was doing.

Four months after my second child, Pierre Ocean, was born, I decided to separate from my husband. I wanted to live life on my own terms and take my kids with me. It wasn't an easy decision, because it's never easy becoming a single mom. I also decided to go full-time as an entrepreneur because it was the only option to free up my time as a mom and not be working full-time or lots of hours while the daycare raises my kids. If I was going to live life on my terms, this was part of it.

I stopped freelancing, and the opportunity came to me to work for a local consulting business doing their social media and email marketing. I was elated, established my business with the state, and then a few months later, COVID-19 hit. While everyone else was hurt, I kept the faith and saw profits coming in left and right because I was already running an online business. The government loans and grants helped other businesses continue to run, and they were able to pay me to do work for them.

I was working but still neglecting myself. I began creating a better life for myself but not where I wanted to be.

Business owners must not neglect thy self, lest something dies – either the business or the owner.

## The Ebb and Flow

My decision to live life on my terms came with a cost. I had to work on finding myself. I worked with a therapist and some life coaches to help me understand emotional intelligence and help my mental game get stronger. A lot of inner healing took place, and I have learned to look at life subjectively. I found out I lost myself after marriage and kids. I took care of everyone else but myself. I lost friends because I stayed in an unhealthy marriage and they didn't support any of my business endeavors. I lost my will to dance as my freedom of expression. I grew a resentful and bitter heart because of the life I created for myself to feel accomplished and get things completed by certain ages. Also, I didn't feel supported, and I couldn't express myself to anyone. As I continue to learn about emotional intelligence, to be okay feeling and doing the things I want to do, I see this as my authentic self.

Remember earlier when I was in the car, and there was a colleague trying to reach me, but she couldn't cause I refused to answer her call? Well, today, that colleague is my coach, and she is helping me take my mindset and my business to the next level. She gave me the assignment to have my family and friends answer some questions. She called it "feedback questions." I couldn't be too shocked because what they saw is what I presented to them, but I knew that wasn't really who I was. I realized I was living inauthentically for a long time.

I am now committed to living authentically and purposefully, and helping others do the same using biblical principles. I saw I created an inauthentic life, but now I am creating an authentic life, full of love, abundance, and ready to help transform others' lives.

Putting God first is the only way.

As a result of living authentically, I am really creating healthy patterns for my marriage family, and finally have a real vision and am now aligning my business with my personal core values. I have established boundaries and got rid of people pleasing. I now coach online and offline experts on how to establish and streamline their marketing efforts using social media and other online methods. I get to help authors market their books. I get to see business professionals increase their revenue by helping them create authentic content for their online presence. I also see people's mindset transform in my program, **Social Secrets that Convert**. People have said they went in for a marketing strategy and came out a whole new person.

# Dare Not to Neglect Thyself

## Life Lessons to Live by

### Lesson #1 – *Self Care*

You must pay attention to yourself. Find out what grounds you. For me, it's nature and water. If I can walk on a trail or get immersed in some water, I find it helps me think clearly, frees me from thinking too hard, and my energy resets. Once every 30 days, I plan to carve out 24 hours to be all by myself. I am currently building up to that point. I use this time to reset my energy and do things I want or eat what I want. Most importantly, I spend lots of time with God to get clarity and guidance on my next steps in life. I used to think self-care was external, like getting my hair or nails done, but it's really taking care of the inner self: mental, emotional, spiritual, and financial.

### Lesson #2 – *Feeling Accomplished*

It's okay to want to feel accomplished. It's okay to think highly of yourself and walk in that, but do not do activities or be involved in organizations for social status. I wanted to get married right after I graduated college, travel around the world as an influencer, and I didn't want kids until I turned 30. I couldn't travel because I never made enough money to do it. I did get married after college and had my first child at 30. The overarching concept here is I didn't have a real vision or plan I stuck to. Ultimately, I created a life with lots of detours and never got back on track until now.

### Lesson #3 – *Answer the Call*

You have to know when to answer the call. It just may change your life. There are door-knocking opportunities, and there are once-in-a-lifetime opportunities. Someone once said, "When opportunity knocks, answer." This is true for every situation in life. Open your mind up enough that when you get offered an opportunity to change something about your life or your mindset, you can do it with no issues or delays.

### Lesson #4 – *Don't Harbor Offense*

Whenever someone did something I didn't like, I took offense at it and cut them off. If someone didn't like my spouse or my business, I cut them off. When someone said, "I don't even know why she had another baby by him," and didn't tell me that but told someone I don't even know, I cut them off. I mean, I know people talk about people behind their backs, but never did I ever in life believe that someone said something like that about me! That action was beneath me. And because it came from someone in my home church, someone who called me a friend and someone who smiled in my face and held my children, I cut off EVERYBODY! Since no one wanted to tell me the truth, then I removed myself. This ATE ME ALIVE.

If you harbor offense, you are leaving unforgiveness in your heart. Matthew 6:15 says, "But if you do not forgive others their sins, your Father will not forgive you of your sins." Plus, here is a reminder, forgiveness is not for them; it's for you! If I was ever going to get rid of bitterness and resentment, I was going to have to forgive.

# LaMeshia Conley

You will need to do this whether or not the person who offended you is dead or alive.

## Takeaway Summary

- Why did I work a bunch of jobs?
- Who are the best people you should look to get feedback from?
- Why is living an authentic, fearless, and free life your best bet?

## Take Inspired Action

1. **Write out your vision and make it plain.** Put it on your screensavers on all of your devices. Life is multifaceted, and we have multifaceted goals. There are ten domains of life. The areas are Physical, Spiritual, Financial, Emotional, Mental, Marital, Parental, Social, Vocational, and Avocational. Write a vision for each area, and then write 20 things you would like to do in those areas. Write down today's date, and each year on this date, cross off all that you have accomplished in the areas.

   You created the life you have. Now it's time to live the life you want.

2. **Get rid of emotional blocks.** Write down each of these questions on a sheet of paper and use the whole sheet to answer:

   - What do you want?
   - What is in the way?
   - Who is in the way?
   - What happened?
   - How did you feel?
   - What do you want to happen now?
   - Do you need to forgive yourself or others?
   - What is the lesson I learned?

   The more you express, the more you let go. Every emotional block was built brick by brick. And be honest with yourself when you get to the question, "What do you want to happen now?" You will notice you will start to take charge of your mind, and you are retraining your mind on what to do with these experiences. You will see choices, and you will make the choice to change or not.

## Dare Not to Neglect Thyself

If we don't learn the lessons with our experiences, we will repeat them with another person.

3. **Get Feedback.** Feedback will let you know if you are living authentically or not. Find ten of the closest people that know you and will share their honest opinion answering these questions:

    - What is one thing you could come to me on advice about?
    - Name three areas you feel I have been neglecting and could develop more on?
    - What are three things holding me back from achieving more?

Don't get an attitude, don't harbor offense, just take it. This should transform and catapult your personal development.

> *"Business owners must not neglect thy self,
> lest something dies, either the business or
> the owner."*
> ~ LaMeshia Conley

Ya, Girl!

LaMeshia Conley

# LaMeshia Conley

## About the Author

I am **LaMishia Conely**, and I am a content strategist coach for entrepreneurs and CEO of Marketing with Mesh LLC. I have been in marketing for seven years, starting out as a freelancer, but most recently I have been intentional about scaling. I have two degrees, and that's only where my skills come from. I received my experience working with business owners ready to launch or scale their business using automation.

I help to bring change to the lives of others in your circle of influence. Once you work out the mental, emotional, and physical wellbeing, the light is able to shine from within.

Whatever you deem as success will just flow freely, and everyone will see and experience the overflow.

# Dare Not to Neglect Thyself

## Find Me!

### Your Favorite Content Strategist Coach

**Find me everywhere online** *@meshnicci*

**Websites:**

https://www.marketingwithmesh.com

https://www.meshonclubhouse.com

# Disruption to Destiny

## Megan Bruiners
## Purpose Coach, South Africa

*"There is purpose attached to your pain".*
*~ Stephanie Hill Nchege*

## The Disruption

It will happen in God's time...

These were the words that I muttered under my breath every time I was asked when my husband, David, and I began starting a family after being married for seven years. It felt like it was an intrusion, a breach of my privacy as I was compelled to respond instead of being in a room filled with silence. It was a conversation starter for colleagues, acquaintances, and corporate gatherings.

When I got married to David, we were transparent with each other and intentional to share our past mistakes, trials, failures and shortcomings. I struggled with low self-esteem, rejection, shame, identity crisis, approval addiction, fear of judgement, double-mindedness, and doubting my own capabilities for the most part of my adolescence. I was a prisoner of my thoughts, afraid of living the true expression of who I was called to be, always comparing myself to others. I was on a journey of self-discovery in pursuit of my purpose. Comparison kills our joy. Deep down, I wasn't satisfied with the status quo. In my innermost being, I knew there was more. My pain served a purpose!

Three years into my marriage, after a visit to the gynaecologist, we were advised of the discovery of a small fibroid. At that moment, I was afraid that it would affect my chances of conceiving, but I kept the faith. A few years passed, and I felt led to go to my local gynaecologist for a follow-up and found out that it had grown into two huge fibroids. The thoughts that flooded my mind was that this must be happening to me because of the decisions I made in the past. I was fighting the still voice that whispered, *This is part of your testimony*. God turns our mess into a message.

I underwent a successful operation to remove the fibroids during one of the most difficult seasons in my life. My father was diagnosed with stage-four stomach cancer, and I had to prioritise my health while experiencing disruption and emotional turmoil. He passed on a few days after I was discharged from hospital. During my recovery after surgery and four negative pregnancy tests later, I made a decision to put an end to the self-sabotage, negative self-talk and shift my mindset from being overwhelmed by my emotions to where I want to see myself as an emerging Kingdom entrepreneur.

Where the mind goes, the man follows.

## The Transition

Everything changed when I re-directed my energy, time, prayer life and focused on my journey to wholeness. It was a belief problem. Society and the cultural context we grew up in have groomed us to believe that if we are not married at a certain age or don't bear children in the first year of marriage, there must be something wrong. This can be a stronghold (erroneous thought pattern) in our minds. During my transition, when a thought was not in alignment with God's plan for my life, I would cast it down and write down the vision for my life with daily affirmations. Vision keeps us grounded, humble, motivated and gives us the ability to trust the process.

And that's exactly what I did. I refused to nurture my dysfunction and instead believed my Creator's ways were higher than my ways.

## My Entrepreneurial journey

It's been almost a year since I have been retrenched after a successful career as a flight attendant for 14 years. I was literally pushed out of my comfort zone; however, the disruption positioned me for destiny. As I activated my gifts and talents while flying from country to country, it was only dress rehearsals in preparation for the final play. The call on my life was bigger than me. I felt a sense of responsibility as a first-generation serial entrepreneur to change the narrative of writing best-selling books and building five-figure businesses from being the *standard* rather than the *exception*. My entrepreneurial journey was birthed by my passion for travel. After completing my master's degree whilst flying, I ventured into starting my own travel business, Travel Gem, in Cape Town, South Africa, in 2017. But then the pandemic directly affected the travel industry, and everything changed.

I was armed for battle! I have been preparing my exit plan before lockdown started, and it was time for execution. I was awakened to purpose

## Disruption to Destiny

and launched my first book, *Unmasking Purpose*, within nine months after the pandemic started. I was unlocked during lockdown! I pursued coaching and discovered the hidden potential that was always inside of me. I prayed about the brand I wanted to create, how to package myself as an entrepreneur, but most importantly, I prayed for those who I was called to serve. My Kingdom business, Purpose Mid-wife, was birthed during the crisis.

It is during a crisis when new opportunities present themselves.

Yes, it's all around us. You are one step away from financial freedom and being a wealth creator. My faith has been stretched, and I am now helping Kingdom entrepreneurs to boost their confidence, align their business to purpose, and implement strategies to build a profitable online business. This would not have been possible if I didn't invest in a Business Mindset Coach. The investment in my personal development was worth every cent.

The resources we have been given represents multiple seeds that we need to sow in fruitful ground so that it can bear fruit. It relates to stewarding our time well, prioritising important tasks, applying self-discipline, having an attitude of gratitude, and a mindset to succeed.

## The Five Keys for Growth

### Growth Key 1: *Be Purpose-driven*

You do not need anyone's permission to live an authentic life. So many people voice their opinions on what is good for you when it is not necessarily right for you and your unique assignment. Seeking God first and aligning yourself to His will is key as a mother raising children of destiny, as gift carriers, visionaries, and impact leaders in our communities. We have been given gifts, passions and desires to move us closer to purpose. I became intentional to invest my time and focus on my highest values and rearranging the tasks that were less important. Misaligned focus and poor planning are the biggest contributors to procrastination.

Our creativity and ability to innovate is not affected by a crisis. In retrospect, they get unlocked when we are under pressure from our external environment. We adapt and overcome.

Success looks different to everyone. There are no set of rules and timelines to make the first million or a mandatory list to follow. What a relief! Define what success means to you and plan towards it. God has a unique blueprint for your life. You are not competing with anyone but fulfilling your ordained purpose.

If you are not where you want to be, give thanks and take some time out to take a deep breath. *Treasure the in-between moments!* These few words changed my life! Many times, we become so busy striving for perfection when we should be enjoying **now**.

There is power in waiting your turn and celebrating others around you. How is your attitude while you are waiting?

**Growth Key 2:** *Know your value and worth*
Ten years ago, I never knew my worth and believed the lie that I needed to fit in to be accepted. It was a limiting belief that stemmed from my upbringing, cultural beliefs, and generational line. For instance, the limiting belief why many never write a book is because they don't know where to start, not feeling worthy of writing one, and the fear that nobody wants to read their story because it is not significant. Another limiting belief is that we are not creative. If we serve a God who is creative, so are we.

We are made in the image of God and have His nature. He validated us before anyone had an opinion. We are His Masterpiece. When you get a revelation of who you are, that you are fearfully and wonderfully made, then you will walk a little bit taller with confidence. Your worth is not determined by your mistakes, what others have done to you, or your imperfections.

When you work for an employer, they can never pay you for what you are worth, only their perceived value of you. As an entrepreneur, your clients pay you for your time. Your value supersedes any transaction.

Strive for excellence in all you do and remove yourself from circles that don't want to see you prosper. Not everyone is meant to go with you into the next season.

**Growth Key 3:** *You will never feel ready*
If we want to be successful and realise our dreams, we need to get out of our feelings. Not managing our emotions never serves us well. When I was presented with unfamiliar terrain, I decided to control my feelings and "Do It Afraid". Nothing grows in the comfort zone, and if we are going to take a step of faith, there is no room for overthinking. My "why?" kept me focused and helped me to push the boundary of fear. My convictions were bigger than my fears! I overcame my fear of lack, fear of the unknown, fear of rejection, and the fear of what people will say.

As trailblazers, Kingdom ambassadors and ambitious women on a mission, we need to be comfortable with being uncomfortable. Some people think about chasing their dreams, some talk about them, but a few have the courage to get things done and pursue them. Excuses can't give us the desired results. We need to own every missed opportunity and take action. The moment I showed up consistently, regardless of how I felt, I started making progress.

**Growth Key 4:** *It's bigger than you*
The business you are running is bigger than you, the call on your life is bigger than you, and the responsibility of raising world changers is bigger than you. There is a battle for your seed, time, resources, focus and destiny. If you don't have a written-down vision for your life, you will lack the tenacity to see it through. Your faith will be tested, you will endure a season of crushing, rejection, betrayal, and your integrity will be challenged. You are more than an

# Disruption to Destiny

overcomer, and these trials were not designed to kill you but to strengthen you. If you can put yourself where you see yourself in relation to the vision God gave you, you can use it as the compass that guides you towards your destiny. Your vision and values are power tools that will catapult you towards success. I have also discovered that if we do not believe bigger, we can't receive bigger.

Don't be too hard on yourself when you fail. It's only an event and doesn't define you. Forgive yourself if you allowed failure to form a mental blockage preventing you from dreaming big. Ask yourself what the lesson was, and move forward from there. When we take accountability for our actions, we make room for a fresh understanding as well as knowledge and insight to flow.

What is the legacy you want to leave behind for your children and the next generation?

### Growth Key 5: *Set boundaries for yourself*
Your emotional, mental health. and peace are your personal power. Protect them at all times, no matter what. Toxic relationships, environments, and conversations can kill your destiny. Be mindful of negative self-talk and the controlling behaviours of others.

> "Guard your heart, for everything you do flows from it."
> ~ Proverbs 4:23

We should keep our hearts pure and not allow bitterness to torment us. It keeps us in bondage. On my journey of being a "mom-to-be", my greatest lesson was to "just be" and to not allow anyone to impose their false beliefs and expectations on me.

Our soul consists of our mind, will, and emotions. The well-being of our soul is determined by our emotional health, thoughts we meditate on, and how we process hurt and unhealthy desires. When you do not confront toxic relationships, controlling behaviour, and break the pattern of limiting beliefs, your soul can't prosper.

We are spiritual beings with a soul, in a physical body.

## Transforming pain into power

God is no respecter of persons. You can be anything you decide to be. Destiny is determined by your decisions. Think of it this way, your future has already been prepared for you, but you need to walk in it and believe you deserve it. I am believing with you. What do you do when your prayers are left unanswered?

You give it all you got; walk by faith and not by sight!

I am expectant for great things: to reach my full potential as a Kingdom entrepreneur, to impact lives one story at a time, and to leave behind a generational blessing for my children. I see myself as a wealth creator, empowering thousands of women, mentoring the future generation, helping those struggling with shame to discover their purpose, and flowing in my prophetic anointing to break mental strongholds.

Wealth is an idea; it is not necessarily material things! You can have spiritual wealth, physical wealth, social wealth, and generational wealth. When you look at your life, what do you see?

God makes provision for the vision! Remember, it's not about you but the people you are called to.

You were destined for greatness, not barrenness. You are anointed for overflow, not a financial low. You have a sound mind, so let anxiety and worry go. You were destined to thrive and not merely survive.

You are a destiny carrier.

## Action Plan Steps

### Step 1: *Get clarity on your purpose*
You were born with a purpose which is the original intent for what you were created. The grief you endured, the business that you lost, children that rebel, financial struggles, emotional turmoil, and addictions all point you to your purpose. Yes, that's right. You have been graced to help victims of abuse because you overcame it. It happened **for** you, not to **destroy** you.

What comes naturally to you, what brings you great joy and are the things that your friends compliment you on, have always been there, but you need to be intentional to express them in your daily life. You are a vessel and expression of God's redeeming love and saving grace.

### Step 2: *Get clarity on your calling*
Say "Yes" to the call. You have gifts inside of you to solve a problem in society. Not everyone is called to preach; however, we have a role to play, whether it's through giving, exhortation, speaking, being a marketplace leader, writing, or operating in our gifts. We can desire gifts from above to complete our God-given assignments, and He will give them to us if it's in alignment with His will. We do not ask; therefore, we do not receive. Your gift will make room for you.

### Step 3: *Invest in your personal development*
You are your biggest asset. Invest in workshops, conferences, and programs that will help you in getting the desired results. You need the knowledge, expertise, and experience of someone that has been where you desire to be. You can't use the same strategy and expect different results. Find a coach you are compatible with and do whatever it takes to start working on shifting your mindset. You don't need to spend years figuring it out for yourself.

In this new season, a new strategy is required. Make a commitment to your future self that you will not be controlled by a scarcity mindset and transition into living a life of abundance. When you adjust your mindset, you change your life. Prioritising self-care is key.

## Disruption to Destiny

I wrote a letter to my younger self, broke ties with my former self and declared what is to come. We speak these things into existence as if they already are. Our words carry power.

It is a privilege to empower aspiring and emerging Kingdom entrepreneurs and to assist them in aligning their business to purpose. If you want to do a career change and pursue your coaching business, you can. If you want to pay off your debt and have financial freedom, you can. If you desire the gift of writing and want to become a bestselling author, you absolutely can! It is all up to you.

As I am evolving into motherhood, my assignments and the audience I serve may change, but my mandate stays the same – to impact one life at a time with my story. I am living in my purpose and helping countless women discover theirs.

And, so can YOU!

*"Your story has the potential to set someone free
who has become a prisoner of their own thoughts
and a victim of their circumstances."*
~Megan Bruiners

Destiny Carrier, Do it Afraid!

*M C. Bruiners*

Your destiny helper,
Megan Bruiners

# Megan Bruiners

## About the Author

My name is **Megan Bruiners**. I am an ordained prophetess, Kingdom entrepreneur, purpose coach, and TV program host of "Changing the Narrative with Megan Bruiners". I am also the founder of an online coaching business, Purpose Mid-wife, where I help aspiring and emerging Kingdom entrepreneurs to unlock their hidden potential, get clarity on purpose, and walk in their calling confidently so that they can build profitable businesses with lasting impact. My corporate mission is to help Kingdom coaches, consultants, authors, and online service entrepreneurs to transform their pain into purpose by rewriting their story with God as they influence societies with their gifts.

It is truly an honour to partner with God and witness women saying "yes" to the call on their lives.

I love date nights, walks on the beach, Thai cuisines, and travelling off the beaten track.

Yes, I am now an **ambitious mama-to-be**!

Afterall, God's time is perfect…

# Disruption to Destiny

# Find Me!

*Facebook*: https://www.facebook.com/PurposeMid-wife

*Instagram*: https://www.instagram.com/purposemid_wife

*YouTube* **(Changing the Narrative episode):**
https://youtu.be/GeXF6ln4ISg

**Email:** PurposeMid-wife@safrica.com

**Schedule a Free 30-minute Purpose Clarity Call (1:1 coaching):**
https://calendly.com/megancbruiners

# Decision-Making to Decision-Acting

## Mika Thornton
## Co-Founder of Tendo Ministries, Uganda, East Africa/ Alabama, USA

*"When you start letting yourself be your biggest motivator instead of your biggest critic, you find yourself more willing to make decisions that catapult you forward into who you always wanted to be."*
~ Mika Thornton

## In the Beginning...

For a long time, my life has really been one giant oxymoron, but especially in regard to what I wanted to do with my life post-graduating college. As an international nonprofit founder at 19, I longed for nothing more than to eventually graduate college and move to Uganda to continue the work I had started every summer of my college career, but on a full-time scale. I spent a lot of my time throughout my school years trying to figure out how I could function in Uganda as a full-time volunteer with no consistent form of income but also pay off over $100,000 in student debt. Yep, there's the oxymoron part.

I remember the conversation that triggered a change in my perspective. In my sophomore year, I attended a weekly meeting with one of my professors. On this particular day, I had just booked a flight to Uganda for my second service trip for the summer of 2017. I had planned to stay the entire summer instead of just the short two weeks I had committed to the year prior. During my first summer in Uganda, I realized a handful of things. First, only being in a different culture for two weeks doesn't actually allow you to be immersed in the traditions, learn the language, and get to know the place and its people properly or intimately. Second, the impact of a short-term trip could sometimes be more harmful than good (take a look at Brian Fikkert's *When Helping Hurts*). Lastly, Uganda was where I wanted to be. It didn't matter if I was needed there; I just *wanted* to be there.

## Mika Thornton

As I rounded the corner into his office that day, my professor immediately knew that something weighed heavy on my mind and that I wasn't there to discuss my grades. I spilled out my passion for Uganda and why I hated being in America when I felt like I could be enjoying my life so much more working alongside Ugandans in their communities.

"So, just drop out and go," he advised with a shrug. I gasped for a breath in shock as I sought further clarification.

"What do you mean? I can't just MOVE TO AFRICA? I'm a college student..."

My professor's next monologue quite literally shook me to my core. I won't attempt to quote it directly, but the content included arguments that as cliche as it is, life is just too short to not only miss opportunities but to make yourself miserable thinking about all of the ways every opportunity could end sourly. The basic principle is, just do the damn thing! He instilled a knowledge in me that following the pattern of life that everyone else follows is boring and anticlimactic. Doing the crazy while you're young, like moving to Africa with no plan, was the kind of crazy thing he said he wished he'd done as a young 20-something. I couldn't believe my professor was encouraging me to drop out of college and move to the other side of the world over an afternoon chat.

"This is the greatest time in your life to make it happen. You're not married, you haven't started a career, you're basically free to make decisions, make mistakes, and have a damn good time doing it," he would go on to say.

Little did he know those words would shape my entire decision-making process in every aspect of my life for years to come.

## It Didn't Go Down Like That

Quick spoiler alert for you: I, in fact did *not* take my professor's advice that day, but the thought of what my life could have been eventually caught up to me. I spent the next three years traveling back and forth to Uganda each summer, trying everything I could to be a college graduate and get to move to Uganda to volunteer full-time. It seemed every time I revisited the idea, it was quickly shut down due to a lack of funding. I just continued to work on school, manage my nonprofit from afar, and hope that something bigger would come one day.

I think all of us get into that sort of comfortable place where we realize that if the thing we truly want doesn't occur in our timing, it just isn't meant to be, and we begin to plan otherwise. This was definitely the case for me. I began to be okay with giving up my dream of spending extended time in Africa. I got a corporate job, lived in a ridiculously expensive apartment, and just did what many other fresh college graduates did – I settled.

## It All Clicks

Until that is, out of nowhere, someone I trusted presented me with an

# Decision-Making to Decision-Acting

opportunity. Their words: "I want you to go to Uganda. We can make it happen. Trust what God has for you there and that He will provide, and just go and be where you know you're meant to be."

I heard the words of that professor echoed in my life through this trusted person, and that night, I informed my dad that I would be moving to Uganda sometime in the next six months, and I had the entire next three years planned out by sunrise. I'm not sure what changed in me. Maybe it was my youthful heart regretting the previous time I was presented with this notion and I shut it down, but this time, I was going to go, and no one was going to change my mind or my heart. I knew that I would likely never have an opportunity to grab a chance like this again, and by God, I was going to take it and not let go.

In the following weeks, I informed friends and family of what was to come, and somehow, enough money for me to move to Uganda and live there with no worries for three full years appeared in my possession. I can't tell you that I had anything to do with it except for my willingness to trust that this was the time to jump.

## Moving Forward: On the Equator

What I *did* plan for, however, was how my time in Uganda would be used to help and not hurt. As I sit here over a year later at my dining room table in my Ugandan home, there's still a lot of work to be done, but I'm excited about the directions the work I get to do is going. Two Ugandan mothers and their children live alongside me in my home to grow in their skills to become independent. We are working towards a self-sustaining school system, providing work opportunities to the village families we serve, and my ultimate goal is to eventually be able to hand over this entire organization to my Ugandan co-founders, and I just get to be a visitor. I'm also in the process of adopting my two little girls, something that would have never been possible had I not made the move to Africa. I'm now a mom, a friend, a leader in my community, and most of all, happy!

## How Does this Apply to Every Woman?

### Lesson 1: *Just Be Crazy*

There are things that people will call you crazy for, and then there are things that YOU will call you crazy for. I can promise you this: if you're going to be crazy, it is so much more fun and satisfying to do the latter. Everyone I talked to about my decision to move across the planet wanted to know, "Why are you wasting your college degree to be a volunteer?" and "How can you do that to your dad?"

All of these questions, although valid to an extent, were centered upon what other people think of me and my decision, not on what I want or think for myself. When I decided to choose myself and what I wanted and do that crazy thing my heart longed for, that is where I found my happiness, my purpose, and my true self.

Also, having children, a marriage, or anything else that demands your attention does not need to be an excuse you use to hold yourself back. In fact, it should be the very thing to catapult you forward towards your dream.

**Lesson 2:** *What Is Meant for You Will Always Be Yours*

No matter what your deity, belief system, or morals and values are based on, whatever the universe has for you will find you. There may be days where you will need to make a decision to trust yourself and/or your higher power to lead and guide you to the very thing that is meant for you, but at the end of the day, you'll find yourself exactly where you're supposed to be. I know this cliche is often overused and underappreciated, but it really is when you realize this concept and truly believe it that the trajectory of your life and where you're meant to be is not an anxiety-ridden thought process but a hopeful look to the future.

**Lesson 3:** *You Are Your Biggest Fan AND Biggest Enemy*

If you find yourself being held back by something, chances are, you are the one to blame. Often, when we want to make something happen, the only thing holding us back is our inability or lack of motivation to act on it. Instead of thinking, *What is everyone else going to think of this decision?* or *What will I miss out on if I stray from the norm?*, think things like, *What will I be holding myself back from if I don't jump on this opportunity?* and *If I could see myself in a year or two after making this decision, would I be proud of the woman I find there?*

When you start letting yourself be your biggest motivator instead of your biggest critic, you find yourself more willing to make decisions that catapult you forward into who you always wanted to be. Embrace that woman, nurture her, and let your inspiration be who you want to be, not someone else. You'll never be anyone but yourself, so you might as well aspire to be your future self anyway.

**Lesson 4:** *If You're Smart, You Don't Make Excuses, You Find Solutions*

Going along with the previous lesson, excuses are just something to get in the way of your success. For me, it was always "I don't have the funds" or "I won't be using my degree." What needed to happen in my life was a reshift in focus. I needed to look at what *could* be done, not what couldn't. When I reshifted to this mindset was when I found myself realizing just how possible my wants and dreams were. That being said, my shift in perspective allowed me to stop focusing on the excuses I could make to not make something happen, but rather the solution I could find to my problems as a whole.

## Where Are They Now?

At this point, I've found my way to Uganda. I *did* have to wait a long year to make it here due to COVID-19, but in October of 2020, I boarded a plane with ten pieces of luggage to fly halfway around the world, and after over a half

## Decision-Making to Decision-Acting

a year in country, I can honestly tell you I don't think I've ever been more sure of where I was supposed to be than where I am right now.

I'm in the middle of an adoption process. I have some of my best friends here in Uganda living with me along with their children, so life is an everyday bout of chaos that I embrace and love with all of my being.

Over the next year, the Ugandan women I work and live with and I will be opening a sewing and trade school here in Uganda, and alongside each other, we'll be leading women to become the greatest version of their entrepreneurial selves. We hope and pray to grow a ministry that empowers local women to provide for their families and allows them to be connected to other women all over the world in entrepreneurial partnerships and friendships.

Life, especially where we're supposed to be, isn't always written out, planned, and handed to us in a manual. Most times, it's up to you to write the manual and prayerfully hope that the manufacturer is there to come through with the appropriate tools.

Maybe for you, the first step is to pick up the pen.

## Story in Review

To close out, here's a review for yourself of my journey:

1. Do you have an example of someone in your life who has spoken words of wisdom that completely changed your outlook on things like what Dr. Griffin did for me?

2. What experiences are you holding yourself back from by living by what limits you?

3. Do you think that the you that was five years ago could see you now would be impressed or proud of what you're doing?

## Where Do You Go From Here?

1. Be willing to adjust: No great adventure ever starts with inaction or being comfortable. It takes being willing to step out of your zone of comfort to simply find a new one. Maybe you're struggling to make a life-altering decision in your business, your life, or your household. It's time to stop being worried about how uncomfortable you'll be if this change comes, and start thinking about how uncomfortable you could be if you don't do it.

2. Be the woman who inspires you! There's no need to look to other people and compare your story to theirs. Your two life experiences and circumstances can never be the same. For me, I was constantly comparing myself to others' journeys and letting what they were doing

## Mika Thornton

hold me back from being where I wanted/needed to be. I didn't need to compare myself to them and their journey, but I needed to compare my current self with who I wanted and aspired to be. I don't want to be the next (insert inspiring woman here). I want to be the first Mika Thornton.

When I learned this is when I sought happiness in myself and no longer in how proud or impressed others were in me. Finding this balance is one of the happiest places you'll ever be.

*"Making a decision is easy; acting on it is when the real adventure begins."*

Go girl; be who you always wanted to be.

Yours,

*Mika*

Mika Thornton

# Decision-Making to Decision-Acting

## About the Author

Hey there! I'm **Mika Thornton**, and I'm so excited to have been able to share a small piece of my story with you. I'm a co-founder of Tendo Ministries, a Uganda-based organization that serves the people of Uganda and strives to make them self-sustaining and entrepreneurial. I currently live full-time here in Uganda with my friends, Viola and Mary, and their children.

I'm also a business owner of The Terracotta Branch, where I act as a full-time Virtual Assistant, Social Media Manager, and entrepreneur. Some of my favorite things are podcasts, listening and recording, audiobooks, *TikTok*, discovering new places to grab coffee, and just sitting in my hammock on my veranda watching my little farm. Currently (although it could change before the publication of this book), we have two goats, five chickens, a dog, a cat, a hedgehog, five rabbits, and an obnoxious bird that comes by a few times a day.

I'd love to chat with you, so feel free to reach out on my socials for a virtual cup of coffee or just to say "hello"!

# Mika Thornton

## Find Me!

*Instagram:*
    @TerracottaBranch (Business)
    @TendoMin (Non-Profit)

**Website:** TendoMinistries.com

**Email:** mikalatho@yahoo.com

# Consciously Rising

## Natalie Tellish
## Conscious Parenting Coach, USA

*"It is my mission to ensure our children develop a different narrative within--- one of worthiness, empowerment, significance, and unconditional love."*
~ Natalie Tellish, Conscious Parenting Coach

## Vicious Cycle

To say I was exhausted is an understatement. Our kids were taking everything I had to give, plus more. My parenting "style" was "angry" and my one and only tool was *yelling*… well, more like begging and pleading for them to *just* behave. That begging and pleading would become progressively louder and more desperate the more they wouldn't cooperate. I started each day with an exhaustion so deep within me, I am almost certain my spirit alone weighed 100 pounds. Every moment felt excruciatingly hard – like I was trudging through thick quicksand.

*Wake up! Get breakfast ready! God, why were they always so hungry and talkative and energetic as soon as their feet hit the ground?*

Staying home all day, every day, felt like being imprisoned with the same mundane tasks. The way my family was undoing those tasks right behind me felt like some form of sick torture. What had I done to deserve this?

But leaving the house felt harder because getting everyone out the door for a fun outing just to have one of them meltdown in public and feeling all the eyes of people around us staring at us merely confirmed that I was, indeed, on my own. Where was the village?

I had my husband, our four children, and some online friends. That was my village, and my marriage was hanging on by a thread. I felt so far away from my husband. He would go to work, come home, robotically assist with tasks around the house, and help with the kids until their bedtime. We'd go to bed, wake up, and do it all over again. I would talk to him about my dissatisfaction with our life. He'd try to help by offering me moral support, but he genuinely had no idea how to help me work through the challenging emotions I was experiencing.

I didn't know what to do with my overwhelming feelings of frustration. I kept it hidden from the kids as best I could, but they would impact my husband when I couldn't contain them. I knew this was no way to communicate, and his natural response was to shut down for his own safety. My attempts at emotional connection with him were ineffective at the very least, and, over time, they pushed him further and further away from me.

I was truly alone. I had only me and those emotions.

But who had *I* become? This wasn't *me!* I thought. The kids, the house, and my husband had literally *killed* the real me. The *me* that was bubbly, fun, outgoing, spontaneous, cheerful, and radiant was long gone. That previous version of me was *dead*. I had become some zombie-like form of my old self, who could hardly muster up enough energy to get through the task directly in front of me, let alone exhibit any form of fun, cheer, or radiance!

## Eye-Opening Moment

One day, as I stood in our living room, screaming at my husband, I felt my ears pop from the volume of my own voice. I had lost control, as I had countless times before. That pain in my ears snapped me back into reality. Our kids were there, and I could see that they were terrified. My husband felt so helpless that he began to retreat into his shell, as he had done before when I had lost control, then he started to have a panic attack for the very first time in his life. Suddenly I could see what was happening around me rather than only seeing *my* pain.

I had been begging him for years to get our life moving in a direction toward fulfillment and a true loving connection with one another. Something inside of me in that moment whispered, *Why do you think it is his job to give you a fulfilling life?* I felt my heart shatter into a million pieces as I saw my babies and my husband being so negatively impacted by the way I was behaving.

It was at that moment that I realized I had spent years giving away my own power. It hit me that none of my unhappiness was because I had four children under the age of ten or because I had an emotionally unavailable husband. Were those circumstances true? Yes! Did they present challenges in my life? Sure! But I knew at that moment that if I wanted to live a fulfilling life, I had to stop playing the "blame game" and begin taking responsibility for my own joy.

My family deserved better. I deserved better.

# Consciously Rising

## I Finally Had It Figured Out!... Or Did I?

It's not as though I hadn't worked hard for our family up to this point. In fact, I had spent *all* my time thinking about what I could be doing differently. I was constantly planning and implementing new schedules and routines, buying new things for our home to make our life flow more efficiently, and spending time and energy on getting the kids' physical, intellectual, emotional, and spiritual needs met so that they could function at their absolute best. This was the *most* frustrating part. I was doing *all the right things,* and I still wasn't achieving the results I wanted – inner peace, happiness, and authentic connection with my husband and kids.

Day after day, I tried. I tried to wake up each morning hopeful and optimistic that I could be powerful enough to be the driving force in my own life and that I could create joy. By the end of each day, though, I was still going to bed defeated and worn down.

What was missing?

## Healing from the Inside Out

What I discovered was that I had simply been focusing on the wrong things – the things outside of me. I started learning and implementing new parenting techniques, finding new ways to manage my time, making time to play with our kids, investing in my husband's love language, eating healthier foods, and spending more time in nature. These were all great tools that lead to general wellness. However, if a tree is dead at the roots, no amount of water and sunshine will bring it back to life.

Since the beginning of my marriage, I'd known that my husband and I needed to get to know one another's core values and build our life together on a firm foundation of what is important to us. I believe this is the only way to live a truly meaningful life – one in alignment with what has been divinely placed into our hearts. What I hadn't realized was we needed to address deeper issues before we could move forward. My outlook and values had been shaped by the chaos I was raised in. My husband was unable to access his core values because his authentic self had been shut down for a very, very long time. No matter how many incredible efforts we made, our roots were damaged. We needed core healing, not another five-step process to regain control.

## The Power Within

The magic I was searching for was inside *me* all along. The solution wasn't that I needed our kids to behave better or be quiet more often. The answer wasn't that my husband needed to step up and be more emotionally expressive and involved in the planning and managing of our life. It wasn't that I needed to find ways to achieve more each day.

Everything changed when I decided to *choose consciously* to let go of the parts of me that had been programmed from my childhood. The unhealthy patterns that were constantly coming to the surface from inside of me were not simply a response to what was going on around me. They were deeply ingrained within me, having been passed down to me from previous generations. My grandmother was a yeller, my mother was a yeller, and I, unintentionally, became a yeller.

The day I consciously chose to ensure that I did not pass down that pattern, among others, to my children is when I fully regained my power – the power of who I am at my most genuine, core self. The old version of me that I thought had died was merely hidden under years of ineffective coping mechanisms and unhealthy learned behaviors. I had never been taught how to cope with my feelings or how to communicate peacefully in relationships. From a very young age, I witnessed screaming, physical fighting, drinking, and smoking.

It was no wonder I hadn't the slightest idea how to handle the challenging aspects of my life, so    all I had to do was unlearn everything I knew!

## Me, Myself, and I

Once I'd made the conscious choice to become my own, authentic person, rather than continue down the path of emotional and familial destruction, it was time for *conscious connection* with the core of my being. I had to get in touch with the real parts of me, and I had to be intentional about being aware when unhealthy patterns would pop up. I had to pay close attention to my thoughts, feelings, attitudes, and beliefs so I could sort out which were mine and which had been passed down to me through trauma.

It took time and practice to learn new ways of thinking, feeling, and responding to the world around me. At the beginning of this step in the process, I had to look at situations in retrospect after the negative emotions had dissipated. I was still yelling, but once I was able to calm down, I apologized and reflected on what had happened. I analyzed each episode thoroughly to determine where the response within me was coming from and how I could have responded more gently. Most importantly, I had help from coaches who supported me through rough moments, helped me process everything, and made a game plan for the next time a similar situation came up    .

Over time, I began responding the way I desired, planned, and practiced even in the most heated moments. Sitting with my own feelings and working through them during the elevated times was, and still is, key.

## The Real Fun Starts

Once I was able to consciously connect with myself and the people around me, that's when life became *amazingly* fulfilling. I was no longer trudging through the quicksand! I was floating and flying and having an incredible time consciously creating the life I wanted. Through this process, I was able to realize my dreams once again and reignite the fire I'd had for my

# Consciously Rising

life!

Instead of angry outbursts or short, grumpy responses, our kids are now met with silliness and energetic fun. And guess what? Because of the energy I bring into the atmosphere in our home and family, our children are more cooperative than ever before. Their cups are naturally filled, and they're learning effective communication skills by seeing them modeled by their parents. My husband and I no longer have that distance between us. We enjoy one another and the life we are living. Shifting my focus to my own inner healing and growth gave him the space and freedom to begin exploring those things for himself.

With all the mental space and clarity that I gained, I've gone back to college and even launched my own business. I'm truly living the life of my dreams, and it's all thanks to one conscious choice I made and saw through to completion.

## Your Path to Healing, Inner Peace, and Happiness

I have shared a few of the ways my life has improved since implementing these strategies. Now it is your turn! What I did can be applied and practiced by anyone seeking change. With time and consistency, you'll notice incredible enhancements in your life.

1. Consciously Choose to take charge of your happiness. No matter how terrible your circumstances, there are baby steps that can be made to progress in the direction you want your life to go.

2. Consciously Connect, first with your authentic self and your divine purpose. From here, you can sort out what patterns you'd like to keep and which you'd like to leave behind. Which ones are no longer serving you? This can lead to genuine connection with the people that you love most. The relational conflicts and struggles you're currently facing will lose power, and you'll move into a much deeper understanding of your relationships with other people.

3. Consciously Create the life you desire based on your own core values and desires. When you begin your healing journey, and you learn and practice emotional intelligence, the people closest to you will naturally learn as well. When your core relationships are not in pain, turmoil, and strife, you'll have a new space and energy for going after your own dreams and living out your passion and purpose.

With love,

**Natalie Tellish**

Natalie Tellish

# Consciously Rising

## About the Author

I'm **Natalie Tellish**, a certified conscious parenting coach. I have studied, practiced, and taught conscious parenting strategies for more than a decade.

I currently reside outside of Pittsburgh, PA, USA, with my husband and our four children – Josie (12), Sawyer (7), Carver (6), Beric (3). Together, we enjoy day trips, movie nights, campfires, and hikes through the woods.

My passion is helping families connect more deeply with one another, cultivate trust and inspired communication within their homes, and move through life's toughest challenges with poise and confidence. I officially launched my parent coaching business in 2018 and have helped hundreds of families over the past few years.

# Natalie Tellish

## Find Me!

**Website:** http://consciousparentcoaching.com/

**Facebook:** https://www.facebook.com/ConsciousParentCoaching

**Instagram:** https://www.instagram.com/conscious.parenting.coach/

**LinkedIn:** https://www.linkedin.com/in/theconsciousparentcoach/

## My Gifts to You

### Join the Free Community for Daily Parenting Support
https://www.facebook.com/groups/consciousparenting101

### Free Guide to Stop Yelling
https://gem.godaddy.com/signups/50bd7c3ea02f469ca0037841c45719f9/join?fbclid=IwAR3yC92VAvQgiqLJ45PwOn8OPxNvT5N0yaV2IrnXb-VIIxYVvJo8zi38bmc

# My Perfect, Imperfect Life

## By Rita Miceli
## GIACI – Giving Inspiring Autism Clarity Insight, Canada

*"My son has been my most tenacious teacher."*
~ Rita Miceli

### The Struggle Is Real

My story is like that of so many other mothers, wives, and women who feel the need to strive for a "perfect" life.

I was determined to have it all – success, love, family, and happiness – and it was my responsibility to make sure all of these boxes were checked. It was ingrained in me at a young age that my family's well-being was my responsibility, even if that meant spreading myself too thin.

The exhaustion of it all hit me right after my twins were born.

Life in the hospital had been easy. I had constant support and access to rare adult conversations. All I had to do was push a small button, and a maternity nurse would appear to tend to my every need. The room, though stark and bright, was also free of toys and heaps of laundry nudging me towards the endless work. Other than missing my family, I could have comfortably stayed there for another week, maybe two. This was the closest thing I'd felt to being pampered in years.

Once the twins, Carolina and Maria, and I were home, the monotonous, never-ending days and nights began again. The looping days were both predictable and erratic. Everyone needed to be fed and kept safe but also needed attention at varying times or made one mess right after another. I couldn't escape the chaos, not even into my own mind. Entering my brain space was just as much of a whirlwind, a mess of thought and uncertainty. My mind was the last place I wanted to be. All I could fixate on was the looming question of *What if? What if my newborn twin daughters had autism like my son Giaci had?*

When I looked down into their cribs, they looked *normal* like their three-year-old sister Lauren had. But then again, so did Giaci. Would I recognize the signs faster this time, or would it stay dormant for a year again, waiting for the

# Rita Miceli

perfect opportunity to steal even more from me?

It had already stolen my career goals, furthering my education, and my ability to watch my son hit all the "typical" milestones. Autism stole my husband, John, from me. With the emotional labour on my shoulders, the physical labour fell on John. He worked long hours day in and day out to support us, leaving me to count the minutes until he came home.

It would be 960 minutes, 960 minutes until I wasn't alone. The countdown began.

I tried to relish in the moments when all four of my little ones were awake. I tried to be the perfect mother who balanced her time equally between vastly different children, all who needed different parts of who they thought I was.

Having four children in the house felt like a mini-daycare but with no support staff. Diaper changes took up the majority of the day. With three children still in diapers, it was a constant rotation of clean, dirty, dirty, clean. Lauren would try her best to engage her brother while I was either changing the twins' diapers, breastfeeding, or putting them in their cribs for naps.

I stole looks at the clock throughout the day, finding myself at the same lull in the day – 800 more minutes.

It had been six months since we'd moved into our new house, and still it was filled to the brim with moving boxes left unpacked. I looked around at them, thinking about how I could have unpacked them while the twins were napping or have Giaci and Lauren help as an activity. They stayed packed.

Every minute that went by felt like that powerful, perfect woman and mother was slipping further away. I tried to find her in the shower. The shower could usually wash away the minutes and bring me back to ground zero. Except now, I had to bring my children into the bathroom with me, leaving little room for an emotional release.

My time of release turned into a time of more control – trying to keep Giaci from running, locking the door to secure his safety, ensuring that the twins were tucked into their infant bucket-style car seats, trying to pass that little bit of control over to Lauren, my eldest, who was already showing signs of a nurturing, maternal instinct. Every time I asked for her help watching over them or to play with them, I wondered if I was priming her for the same life I'd been leading, I couldn't know. All I knew was that I needed five minutes.

But those five minutes were fractured into 30-second fragments of frantically checking behind the curtain, making sure Giaci didn't run.

Keeping eyes on him and the girls at all times was my daily purpose.

I knew mothering would be hard, but nothing like this. In the shower, everything I hid inside would seep through my pores. Every moment of anger dripped out. Every ounce of resentment towards this disorder drained me of the energy I needed to care for my babies.

It did this. *Autism* did this.

## My Perfect, Imperfect Life

I had four beautiful children but felt like I couldn't reach any of them properly. I had an amazing husband, yet we were both going through our own motions, he on his left and I on my right.

There were now 240 minutes. I stayed in the shower a bit longer this time. My head grow dizzier with steam, taking me away – taking me away from the powerless fight against autism, a foe that was becoming stronger every day.

I watched as Giaci was being pulled deeper into his own world, coexisting less and less with my own. There was less human interaction and continuous repetitive behaviours. To me, autism and my beautiful little boy were two separate entities – at least, I wished they were. I wanted to separate them. I wanted my son to live in my world with an ability to converse, not this isolated existence.

As the water continued to fall and scald my bare back, I blocked out the playful energy from behind the curtain. I didn't even have the will to be present in my kids' joy, not when we had an unknown entity among us creeping in between – a thief who'd come in the night and robbed me of my perfect boy, leaving me with only the outer shell, leaving me with a puzzle gaped with missing pieces, missing parts of him I longed to unlock, taunting me with the fact that I never would.

I started shaking with insurmountable anger brewing inside of me as I shut that water off and dressed myself from behind the curtain. I shouldn't have let this happen. As his mother, I should have fought this disorder away. It was my job, and I'd failed.

I'd failed to keep my perfect life, failed to save us from this. I allowed autism to steal our happily-ever-after, steal all of our potential, leaving us with a blank slate. I spent all day trying to fill the slate with as much information as I could to help my son learn to communicate in our language. My degree as an educator and my drive as a mother charged my desperation to hear my son speak.

*Zero minutes!*

I waited by the door, eager to tell John about our hard day's work, but he was filled with the exhaustion of his own full day.
John was home, but I still felt so alone.
I thought about how all of my life, I had willingly consented to my assigned role as the only daughter of Italian immigrants. I complied with the expectations that came with that role, following every tradition and religious and cultural ritual, believing that if I strived for perfection, I would be rewarded with happiness.

## An Awakening from Within

So, why wasn't I happy yet? Hadn't I done everything right? The way I was told to?

I was watching my life through someone else's eyes – a pair of judgmental eyes that couldn't see beyond the faults of her life. It was as if I'd been locked behind that gaze, chained in place and unable to shift or wake. It wasn't until we nearly lost Giaci that I woke the hell up.

One night, my worst fear came to life. Giaci unlocked the door and ran outside while I'd been flipping the laundry. Any mother could tell you that the split second that it takes your brain to register that your child is missing is the longest, most agonizing moment in any parent's life.

With a pounding heart and a screeching voice, I took to the streets to find him. I couldn't run fast enough, couldn't howl loud enough. Every minute he was missing was a minute where I fell deeper into failure, deeper into the belief that this is a punishment of some sort. When the police finally showed up with my son in hand, it hit me. I could have lost him forever.

I had spent months thinking that I could never reach my son in his world, that there would always be a part of him lost to me. But looking at my sweet, giggling boy, who was right in front of me, I could finally see that he was never lost. He was trying to tell me who he was, and he was trying to tell me who I had to be, or rather, who I *didn't* have to be.

I didn't have to be the perfect mother who had control over everything; that road didn't exist. Instead, I forged a new path, one that was built on acceptance. I could see this new road clearly; it was free of judgement, expectations, and denial. It was exactly the route my family and I needed to take, whether others were on board with us or not.

After having retrieved my son from the authorities, I wrapped my arms around his little body, never wanting to let him go. It was at that moment that I rediscovered my maternal strength.

A *resolute* Rita appeared.

## Finding Happiness

From then on, I made a conscious choice to live life through a different set of eyes, ones that looked through the veil of perfection and was comfortable with what she saw. These eyes stopped caring about the negative looks or other people's judgements. I wouldn't continue to allow my son to be victimized by what others thought of him, or even by what I thought of him. For so long, I blamed myself and was consumed by what I call the "What will others think?" syndrome. I worried more about how others viewed us rather than how I viewed myself, my son, and my family. He was my perfect, precious child that I was proud of, and that was all that mattered.

I chose to stop listening to the voices in my head that judged me, my son, and our circumstances. I refused to succumb to guilt, regret, shame, and disappointment. There was nothing to feel bad about; my son was alive and well. *He* was happy. *He* was a gift of all that is good.

# My Perfect, Imperfect Life

Once I made this mental switch, the anger and anxiety lessened, and the positivity strengthened. I wasn't consumed by sadness and depression anymore. Instead, I was filled with the excitement of cherishing each day. I chose what thoughts would occupy my mind. I chose to be excited about living in the moment with all of my children. I applied that philosophy to every minute of every day. As a result, I was able to have clarity. I was more productive, focusing on the skills my son needed to attain, like language and adaptive skills, instead of the what-if's. I accepted that we were *good enough*, all of us – Giaci, the girls, John, and I.

We were enough, and that was perfect in its own way.

I banished resentment, welcoming in unconditional love and understanding. It was important to be a good example for my daughters. I didn't want them to live a life where they tried to achieve the unachievable. Instead, I taught them that they were all special, that they were loved unconditionally without expectations, judgement, or limitations. They were loved as they came, in this moment. They didn't have to wait for my love and approval.

With these changes came a new richness to my relationship with my husband. Instead of thinking of the *quantity* of time together, we focused on *quality* and the reality that we were both doing our best to cope with our situation – and that was good enough. Love of family was our driving force. I was able to see the sublime commitment of a dedicated father and husband working hard to provide his family with the necessities and care that was needed. He saw the strength and love of a mother who would stop at nothing short than to see her family flourish. Our goals aligned, and our focus was clear – to turn everything we experienced into a gift and opportunity.

As my children grew, my daughters rejoiced in watching their brother gain skills. They were his biggest cheerleaders, and he motivated their emerging characters, which were abundant in compassion, patience, and unbiased endless love.

My previous actions of disillusion were justified by the lies I heard: that I wasn't good enough, that my son was not good enough, that as his mother, I had to fix everything, even if I couldn't control it. I thought I had to please everyone before pleasing myself.

All lies.

I jeopardized taking care of my emotional and physical needs, which led to resentment and burnout. It led to constant frustration and disappointment with myself and others for not living up to the ideal standards I held. I micromanaged every bit of our lives to restore order in my life. The mindset that if I worked hard enough to make my son's inappropriate behaviours disappear was false and only created high anxiety for me, for my children, and my family. But I was afraid of failure for myself and my family. I feared the vulnerability of releasing myself to a life that I didn't envision for us.

The reality of it all was that the controlling thoughts controlled me. They trapped me in my own solitary world. Giaci wasn't the one who was locked up; it was also me. I was lost in this solitary world of expectation, not wanting my son's or my own inabilities to be seen. I thought a perfect life would bring me happiness, but happiness is what I choose it to be. I had the power to seize my happiness in my perfect, imperfect world.

What is perfection, and why did I strive for it? Why do any of us strive for a perfect life? We have a misconception of, *Once I have everything that I dream of, I'll be happy one day.* Yet, even if all of our dreams and desires are attained, will we be happy? Or will we then just try to reach the next level of unattainable perfection?

No, this isn't what happiness is. My son showed me what true happiness is. He has taught me that every little accomplishment has the greatest joy and value. Yes, I had to wait longer than most for my son to say the words I waited for, "I love you, Mommy," but when he finally did, the joy and fulfilment I experienced was more than enough. It was everything!

Finding happiness within ourselves is what brings happiness. Loving myself and who I am, loving my son and who and how he was – this was truly loving. This was living. This was acceptance. Living a beautiful life is savouring every moment instead of waiting to catch that next best thing that never satisfies us because... it is never enough.

It's okay to not be able to see the light at the end of the tunnel because everything will work out even if it's not perfect or how you envisioned it to be. The perfection of life is in how you view it, tackle it, and enjoy it.

It – and you – are enough.

*Following are notes from the author on what to do when your child is diagnosed, you feel the pressures of perfection, or when you need to know that you're not alone.*

1. **Before you can help your child, you need to help yourself.** It's like they say on the plane, "Secure your own oxygen mask first!" If you are taken care of, you'll be able to better take care of your child and family.

2. **Change your perspective.** The world doesn't have a great track record of being accepting or inclusive of people with disabilities, but that doesn't mean your child is "wrong." It means the world needs to do some changing in order to be more respectful. This change starts with you and how you handle this diagnosis (and remembering that your child is more than a diagnosis).

## My Perfect, Imperfect Life

3. **Stop judging yourself.** Everyone else may be saying all of the things running through your head, but it doesn't mean you have to join them. Surround yourself with loving and accepting people, both friends and family members, who will be there to lift you up when you can't lift yourself up.

4. **Try to release control.** Life is full of circumstances that feel out of our control. The sooner we can let go of control, the sooner we can enjoy the life we've been handed and not let the good moments pass us by. There are so many good moments, even in times of darkness. Try to focus on those.

5. **Name it.** Believe in the ability to grow and learn by labelling the root of your challenges. Write it down, keep a journal, and breathe through this inner work.

6. **Be a model for others and your children by doing the work yourself.** Normalize learning, making mistakes, failing versus being perfect, and seeking approval from others. Focus on progress instead of final results because we are never finished growing. Savour each and every gift of the day, no matter how big or small. As a result, you will inspire others. It's contagious.

7. **Go easy on yourself.** This is a journey, and you don't have to walk it alone. Seek out others in your community to learn from, to talk to, and to share your story with.

> *"Find your perfect, imperfect life and live it to the fullest."*
> ~ Rita Miceli

You are not alone,

Rita Miceli

# Rita Miceli

## About the Author

**Rita Miceli** is Canadian, born and raised in the province of Ontario. She has been happily married for almost 30 years to her high school sweetheart, John, and is the proud mother of four beautiful children, Lauren, Carolina, Maria, and Giaci. Since her son Giaci was diagnosed with autism, Rita has spent her life advocating for people with autism and continues to bring awareness to their needs and the needs of family members.

Rita is an elementary school teacher, a professor in the Autism and Behavioral Science Graduate Program at St Clair College, and is past-president of Autism Ontario, Windsor-Essex Chapter. Her favourite things are spending time with her family, dancing, playing the piano, and watching videos of her son on his *TikTok* account, which has surpassed 500,000 followers!

Through the power of social media, her family has impacted many who want to learn more about their journey with autism.

# My Perfect, Imperfect Life

# Find Me!

*Tiktok*: @giacimiceli

*Twitter*: @RitaMiceli3

*Linkedin*: linkedin.com/in/rita-miceli-1a583669

*Instagram*: momma.miceli

*Youtube*: @giacimiceli

**Email**: micelirita24@gmail.com

# It's Time to Take that Chance!

## Sara Ruda
## EMT, Nurse, Rancher, Mom, and Wife, USA

*"Change is painful, but not as painful as
being somewhere you don't belong."*
Sara Ruda

EMS is dispatched out to a domestic disturbance that has been reported by a neighbor who heard a couple fighting. My heart begins to race as I grab my radio and head for the truck. I had gone on several of these calls before, but not like this, not where I had so much in common with my patient. I can see the flashing lights of the police car when we pull up to the residence, and I step out to find my patient with bruises up and down her arms and a black eye. As I walk up to the woman, the police are asking her if she would like to press charges, and she refuses. In the past, I would have questioned the choice, but now I understood it from a different angle. I see it from her point of view. What kind of repercussions would there be? She has been convinced that this is her fault to begin with. He just lost his temper, and it won't happen again. Even if she tries to leave, where would she go?

I begin my assessment with introductions, and as we progress, I feel the cruel irony creep up as I offer numbers and flyers to safe houses for victims of domestic abuse. I can sense the hesitation as I check her blood pressure and pulse and recommend she be seen at a hospital. She refuses to be seen, so I have no choice but to let her stay.

As we left the scene, a wave of emotions hit me – anger, anxiety, helplessness. I was just pissed off. I was so close to the breaking point in my own life, feeling stuck in my own abusive relationship, that not being able to help a patient sent me over the edge. Helping patients was what kept me going, the glimmering light in my own dark days. That night felt like a personal failure to me, and things were only getting worse at home.

When the apologies progressed into excuses and reasons shouted that it was my fault it happened, I knew it was time for something to change.

Dr. Veronica Joseph, D.O.M.

Something had clicked. I am naturally such a forgiving and empathetic person, so I was always trying to see it from his point of view but not anymore. I gave my ultimatum that it needed to stop or I was going to leave, which was met by sarcasm and physical "reinforcement," knowing full well that he had control of the finances, and I had nowhere close to go and still go to work. My photo album of old family pictures and select items that were given to me from other countries that my father had traveled to on deployments were promptly destroyed just to make sure his point was made.

I started to slowly save up money, $5 here, $20 there, and hid it at work so there was no way he could find it. I had planned it out in my head that as soon as I had enough gas money to get halfway across the USA, I was going to leave. As the day got closer, I put in my two weeks notice at work and asked them for my last paycheck to be a paper one so I could cash it in person. I got what few things I had, shoved them in the vehicle, and it felt like I couldn't drive away fast enough. I still had to stop and get fuel where he could see me there, the pump felt like it took an eternity, and the "click" made me jump as I was scanning the streets looking for his vehicle to show up.

One last stop to cash my check, then I was not looking back ever again.

As I was walking into the bank, I ran into one of his friends, who just waved and walked away. My anxiety was through the roof at this point, and I was just ready to get out of the area before he found out. I spent the first hour on the road just looking in the rearview mirror waiting for him to show up, but the further I drove, the more relaxed I got, and it was like a weight was being lifted off of my shoulders with every mile. I was still sad about all the personal belongings and pictures that had gotten destroyed, but now I knew things like that would never happen to me again, and I knew I deserved much better.

Growing up in a small town, I was always surrounded by people who looked after one another and went out of their way to help you if you needed it. I grew up in a family of medical and military backgrounds who emphasized helping others while trying to understand what they are going through. I was also taught that you cannot take care of others if you do not take care of yourself first, and that was the lesson I had let slip away until I decided I had had enough. I had gone into survival mode, clinging onto the good calls I would have at work to keep me going, but that is not what we are meant to do, and that is not living. We are meant to live and thrive and help others after we have made sure that we are in the right place and have taken care of ourselves. We owe it to our families, friends, and anyone else in our lives to make sure we do what is best for ourselves.

I never thought this was how I would be returning to my home state, running away, trying to escape a toxic relationship with only a fraction of my belongings. Initially, there was a sense of relief when I realized I wasn't being followed, but then I went numb. It was hitting me now that I had no job, no set place to live, nothing really to my name. My paramedic license had lapsed due to not being "allowed" to attend recertification courses. I hadn't told my family what was happening or for how long. I lived so far away from everyone and did not want to put that stress and worry on them. But I was headed back now... with no real plan except to get as far away as possible.

I ended up finding a place to rent with the help of my family and getting a job with my medical experience. I began to slowly rebuild my life, and there were unexpected hurdles I had to jump over at every turn. My self-confidence was shattered; I second-guessed myself on everything. I was asking for permission to do things that you would just do in a normal routine. I didn't even know what I enjoyed doing anymore. A co-worker suggested that I start a journal to just write lists of things I used to do. Then write a list of what I like about myself. I started to do that every day along with setting small goals to reach by the end of every week.

I was able to slowly build myself back up.

## Take Care of Yourself

You can't help anyone else if you're not taking care of yourself!! This is especially important if you have a family to take care of. They need you not only as a provider, but they look up to you as an example of what they should allow. They need you! ...and YOU need you!

## Appreciate the Little Things

Find things to be grateful for, no matter how small they seem. This small task will make a huge difference in your ability to make it day to day. Even enjoying the pattern of the couch fabric or the bark of a tree outside can help you temporarily detach. Even try and look at your own fingerprint; that alone will show you how unique you are – one of a kind.

## Be Committed

Set goals for what you want to do in life. Start with small goals that lead you to your big one. Once you decide to commit to a big change, stay focused! There will be distractions and emotions, but the temporary pain you go through is worth the peace and calm on the other side of the storm.

I sat and thought about telling this story for a while and if this would be the best place to do it, and the longer I thought about it, the more it made sense that I needed to do this. There are a lot of women out there like me who have felt trapped in a situation where there seems like there is no way out – but there is. There is a way out, and I did it while living halfway across the country from my family.

Dr. Veronica Joseph, D.O.M.

There are so many out there that can push themselves to be strong while staying in a bad situation. I want to be that motivation to help you be strong in finding a way out. There is newfound freedom, self-confidence, and happiness that comes from getting to be your own person again. The whole world becomes an open canvas; the possibilities are endless as to what you can do.

When I made it back to the Midwest where my family was located, I decided to stay in the medical field but decided not to recertify in paramedicine. I found a new interest in archery competitions and became an instructor as well. I love to help others find ways to de-stress and have fun while learning something new. I currently have a page on *Facebook* dedicated to encouraging women and children to get outdoors and learn about wildlife and the importance of conservation. The page is called Sara Rutten Midwest Huntress.

I am back into EMS, a nurse, and also a CPR instructor. My journey has truly been life-changing, and now I can be the patient advocate and help people the way I was meant to from the beginning.

I am now happily married and have a three-year-old son who loves to help on the ranch. You have endless possibilities waiting for you when you find the strength to spread your wings!!

Let's Recap the Highlights of this Chapter:

1. Why do we need to take care of ourselves first?

2. Should we set big goals or smaller goals first?

3. Why do you think it's so important to keep a positive mindset?

**Make Time to Find Positive Things** that happen during the day. You may not have control over very many things, but your mindset is something that cannot be taken away if you choose to keep it. Look around and find things that make you happy, appreciate the little details in nature. You alone have the ability to change your thought process, and if you continue to make time for the little things that make you happy, then your overall outlook on life will improve and will help you become stronger for yourself and those around you.

**Optimism Is Your Best Bet** – One of the hardest things to do when all you hear are negative things is to think positive. As hard as it may be, you must bring yourself to find the good in everything around you. It will be that light for you when all you see is darkness. Every day find three things you are grateful for or three things that make you happy and think about them. Stick with that routine, and it will get you through things you wouldn't think possible.

**Rediscover Your Confidence** – This sounds so straightforward and

## Embrace the Unlimited Opportunities

simple, but it's not. Rediscover interests that you have not had the chance to do whatever they may be. It could be writing, art, or music. You may need to reidentify your passions or interests. Start by writing down what you enjoy, what you enjoyed in the past, things you've always wanted to do, and your positive qualities. Use that as a jumping-off point for following your interests.

Find your group! Spend time with people who will encourage you to be the person you want to be and lift you up. We all have something to offer in this world that no one else can!

Be proud and confident in who you are.

> "We have no power over what happens around us, only how we react to it."

There is hope in change.

Sara M Ruda

Dr. Veronica Joseph, D.O.M.

## About the Author

I am **Sara Ruda**, and I was born in Plainview, TX. I grew up with two younger siblings, a brother and a sister. I grew up in a very close family where we stayed in contact with even second and third cousins.

My father made sure we always ended up living in a smaller community regardless of where we ended up following him as he performed his military duties. I finished high school in the family home town of 300 people in Nebraska. From there, I found myself everywhere from Lexington, Virginia to San Antonio, Texas. I eventually ended up in Metro Atlanta, Georgia where I worked as a Paramedic.

After a failed marriage and an abusive relationship, I found myself back in the Midwest starting over. I became a cardiac tech and was able to continue my education as a nurse. I began to get back into my hobbies and interests of archery and competition shooting which led me to my current husband.

We have a three-year-old boy who loves to help on the ranch and also comes to the station where I work as an EMT.

Embrace the Unlimited Opportunities

# Find Me!

**Find me on *Facebook*!!**

### Sara Rutten Midwest Huntress
https://web.facebook.com/midwesthuntressKS

### Sara Ruda Go Anywhere Activewear
https://web.facebook.com/groups/986648465152086

**Email:** Ruttenmed@gmail.com

*Instagram*: @nebraskahuntress